SUMMER SAIL

Cruising Green Bay's Historic Waters

by

John B. Torinus

LARANMARK PRESS

A division of Laranmark, Inc.   *Neshkoro, Wisconsin*

LARANMARK PRESS

A division of
Laranmark, Inc.
211 Main Street
Box 253
Neshkoro, Wisconsin 54960

First Printing June 1984

Printed by
Worzalla Publishing Co.
3535 Jefferson
Stevens Point, Wisconsin

Cover photo by Rockne Fitzgerald

TABLE
OF
CONTENTS

ACKNOWLEDGEMENTS

Thanks to:

the following friends, photographers, sailors, and others whose help with this book was invaluable, listed in no particular order but to all of whom I am equally grateful.

Chan Harris at the Door County *Advocate*; Roy Lukes, naturalist at The Ridges Sanctuary; Harrmann Studio in Sturgeon Bay; photographer Robert T. McCoy of Wauwatosa; Jim Quinn at the Neville Public Museum in Green Bay; Jim Van Matre at the Visitors and Convention Bureau in Green Bay; son Mark Torinus, editor of the Menominee *Herald-Leader*; the Wisconsin Division of Tourism; and the Michigan Department of Natural Resources. Plus sailing friends George Kress, George Burridge, Louis Straubel, and Bud Parmentier.

And a special thanks to Rock Fitzgerald who provided me with the color photo he took of a sunset at Egg Harbor which appears on the cover.

The photo of the "Green Flash" on the back cover was taken on the shore of Lake Superior, but there are those who say they have seen what the Spanish call *La Crepusculo* at sunset on Green Bay.

Most of the art work was done by Peggy Eagan, my agent and the wife of my publisher, Larry Names, without whose help and encouragement this book would not have seen the light of day.

This book is dedicated to the many patient friends who helped me learn how to sail a boat, a task I am still trying to master. In particular, this includes my wife Louise, my daughters who took sailing lessons at summer camp and talked me into buying my first boat, my four sons who took turns crewing for me until the youngest jumped overboard on a particularly trying day and swam to shore, telling me to "sail your own damn boat." And their spouses, and now my grandchildren whom I am pressing into service as crew mates.

SUMMER SAIL

Cruising Green Bay's Historic Waters

by

John B. Torinus

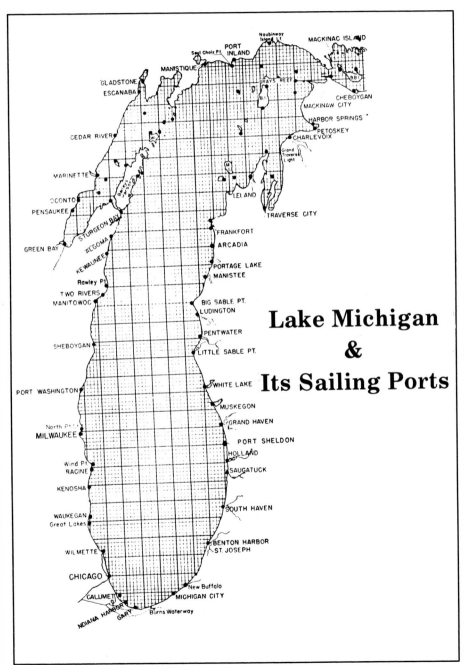

Lake Michigan
&
Its Sailing Ports

INTRODUCTION

A particularly rough, fog-shrouded crossing of Lake Michigan in my sailboat *Cheers* proved to be the genesis of this book. My editor and publisher, Larry Names, was a seasick passenger on the voyage, most of which he spent below decks with his head in a waste basket.

Thanks to our friend, Rob Precourt, who manned the wheel most of the eight hours while I minded the Loran and the charts, we hit Pilot Island at the entrance to Death's Door Passage right on target. The fog lifted when we were about half a mile away and by the time we made the passage into Green Bay waters, the wind had abated and the bay was mirror calm.

With that, Larry emerged from below with the comment, "You should write a book about this."

So I did.

I have spent all my spare summer time in Door County since I was a youngster, and in more recent years, after I acquired a cruising sailboat, a lot of that time has been spent out on the waters of Green Bay. Those hours and days and nights have been so enjoyable that I thought I should share them with other Midwest sailors who might consider a visit to Green Bay waters.

Fortunately, considerable reference material was available, starting with an entire section of the Great

TURNING TO. Author John Torinus (right) and publisher Larry Names tie up the mainsail on the author's yacht *Cheers* after a day of sailing on Green Bay. *Peggy Eagan photo*

Lakes Cruising Club's guidebook dealing with Green Bay. The bibliography will also credit guides to the harbors of Wisconsin and Michigan from their respective tourism departments. Plus a wonderful book on gunkholing on Lake Michigan.

I thought that some of the history of the area would add to a visitor's enjoyment of a Green Bay cruise, and for this I am indebted to Chan Harris, publisher of the Door County *Advocate*, whose grandfather practically built the Sturgeon Bay canal single-handed. Plus historian H. R. Holand and others.

Finally, I picked the brains of a number of my sailing friends, and I was particularly fortunate in that the secretary who transcribes my dictation is married to a sailor, and she is a first class mate herself. Rock and Patti Fitzgerald were valuable critics in getting the book into final form.

THE NIAGARA ESCARPMENT .....

State lines -----

Lake Superior

Lake Huron

Lake Michigan

Wisconsin

Michigan

Ontario

Lake Ontario

Niagara Falls

New York

Illinois

Indiana

Ohio

Pennsylvania

Lake Erie

THE SILURIAN SEA. Millions of years ago the Lower Peninsula of Michigan was under water, a vast expanse known as
the Silurian Sea. The remains of this inland ocean are known
as the Niagara Escarpment, a ridge of limestone that runs
from Niagara Falls along the southern shoreline of Lake
Erie, across the northwest corner of Ohio, through northern
Indiana to the Illinois state line, then north into Wisconsin. It
forms the beautiful and scenic Door County Peninsula of
Wisconsin, the Garden Peninsula of Upper Michigan, and the
islands between the two fingers of land, all of which separate
Green Bay from Lake Michigan. From there it follows the
southern shore of Upper Michigan and the chain of islands
that separate the North Channel of Lake Huron from the
main body of the lake, across Ontario, back to Niagara
Falls. *Map by Roy Lukes*

1

THE WEST CHANNEL

If you and your boat had been around these parts 425 million years ago, you would have enjoyed great sailing on a huge inland tropical sea, the Silurian Sea to be exact, which in that period of geological history, the Mid-Silurian, covered much of the area of the present Great Lakes excluding Lake Superior. Its center was over the present state of Michigan which was a depressed area in that era, depressed physically that is, not referring to the present-day frequent depressions that afflict that state when the automobile business runs into hard times.

A tremendous coral reef was constructed by the many marine creatures that lived in those salt waters and deposited their skeletons on top of each other over a period of millions of years. That reef is known today as the Niagara Escarpment.

This brief sketch of the geological history of the area is essential to your enjoyment of a sailing cruise on Green Bay waters, for it is this impressive limestone ridge which forms the backbone of the Door County Peninsula in Wisconsin, separating the lower area of Green Bay from

Summer Sail 13

Lake Michigan, and also the backbone of the Garden Peninsula in Upper Michigan, which separates the upper end of the bay from the lake.

This same limestone ridge then continues along the north shore of Lake Michigan and into the Lake Huron area where it forms the boundary between the cruising waters of the North Channel and Lake Huron. And just as the string of islands stretching from the Door Peninsula to the Garden Peninsula in Upper Michigan separates Green Bay from the big lake, so do the islands formed by the limestone ridge. Drummond and Manitoulin, primarily, mark the separation between Lake Huron and the North Channel. This extensive limestone escarpment emerges at Niagara Falls and from there dips into New York state. It emerges again at the southwest end of Lake Erie and continues westward through Ohio, into Indiana. That was the southern shore of the Silurian Sea.

These islands and spectacular cliffs along the eastern shore of Green Bay provide a photogenic panorama that adds so much to the enjoyment of cruising the area. The Door County shore of Green Bay is a succession of scenic bluffs and quiet harbors, by each of which a small resort village has developed on the sandy shores.

I was first exposed to this interesting geological history of the Door Peninsula by Roy Lukes, the naturalist at the Ridges Sanctuary on the shore of Lake Michigan near Baileys Harbor.

I was enjoying a week's vacation at a nature school conducted by Roy and his wife Charlotte at *The Clearing* near Ellison Bay in Door County, and on a nature walk along the rocky shore of Lake Michigan at the very tip of the Peninsula, he set the class to searching for coral fragments scattered among the small rocks and pebbles. A light went on in my memory. My family back in the 1930s had built a summer home on the bay side of the Peninsula near Egg Harbor, appropriately named *The Omelet*, and a local stonemason constructed stone walls surrounding the property, walking paths, and a large outdoor grill where the family enjoyed cookouts for many years thereafter. In the center of the chimney of this grill was a large round piece of coral fossil. It always fascinated me, and I presumed the stonemason had secured it from some other area in his rock collecting in those days. When Roy was telling us about the tropical sea, I suddenly realized that that piece of coral fossil had been picked up right on the shore in front of our summer home.

The farmers and orchardists who have scraped a living out of the rocky soil of Door County have piled stones along their fence rows and in large mounds in the center of many of their fields. A sailor who is also a rock hound can spend fascinating hours digging through these piles of rock for various fossils, some of which are tropical in origin. Permission should be secured from the land-owner, of course.

Green Bay is surprisingly similar then to the North Channel in size and as well as geological formation. It is approximately 115 miles long from the mouth of the Fox River at Green Bay to the northern tip of Big Bay de Noc inside the Garden Peninsula, and at its widest point, between the Michigan shore and Rock Island, it is about 23 miles wide. Contrary to the North Channel, however, it runs northeast-southwest, which is of considerable advantage in offering a variety of winds, making for flexibility in charting a sailing course. Prevailing winds are from the southwest, with occasional blows from the northwest which will last two to three days. In hot summer weather, there is the chance of heavy thunderstorms with a possible accompanying line of squalls. Fortunately, these are vivisible at least a half hour in advance, travelling generally from northwest to southeast.

This is in contrast to the east-west orientation of the North Channel with its accompanying westerly winds which generally offer only the two choices of downwind sailing going east or long tacking duels returning to the west.

I have cruised both waters and can truly recommend a sailing cruise on Green Bay as being equally as delightful as one on the North Channel and considerably more handy to get to for sailors from much of the Lake

Michigan area.

There are five entrances to Green Bay from Lake Michigan, beginning with the Sturgeon Bay and Lake Michigan Ship Canal leading from the lake into Sturgeon Bay, then the larger Green Bay waters. This is probably the best choice for any sailor approaching from anywhere on southern Lake Michigan and from points as far north as Leland on the east shore of the lake. It certainly is the preferable entrance from sailors from the Chicago area and any ports along the western shore of Lake Michigan. It is well marked by the lighthouse at the Coast Guard station on the northern tip of land marking the entrance to the canal.

The other four choices lie between the northern end of the Door County Peninsula and the southern tip of the Garden Peninsula.

At the north end of the Peninsula is the Porte des Morts Passage which is again well marked by a Coast Guard station on Plum Island and a lighthouse to the east on Pilot Island. There is apt to be some bad weather in the area and navigators are cautioned to get a good fix on the lighthouse on Pilot Island well before approaching the passage, for there are shallow reefs both north and south, including a very dangerous one off the southeast corner of Pilot Island. An adjustment in course is required to pass safely through the passage. The reefs are all well marked on the charts and a reasonable amount of navigational care will insure a safe passage.

At this point, I might throw in a caution that on at least half of the occasions when I have crossed Lake Michigan I have encountered severe fog problems and many times the sailor encounters pea soup conditions well out into the lake after he has already committed himself to the crossing. Loran or radar equipment will prove most valuable out on the big lake.

The Rock Island Passage is fairly open and well marked. This is less true of the St. Martin Island Passage just to the north despite the fact that this one is marked by a Coast Guard lighthouse station on the north end of the island.

The Poverty Island Passage further north is the least favorable of the four and offers no advantage over the St. Martin Passage for sailors proceeding to either Little or Big Bay de Noc.

One of the problems sailors encounter in approaching Green Bay from the big lake is that there are only two ports of refuge on the west shore of Lake Michigan prior to proceeding on into Green Bay. One of these is at Baileys Harbor halfway between the Sturgeon Bay Canal and the Porte des Morts Passage, and the other is a well protected harbor and marina at the southeast corner of Washington Island known as Njord Heim.

Baileys Harbor presents a bit of a problem for sailors approaching from the big lake, particularly in heavy weather or fog, and though the harbor channel is well marked, it is rather narrow. The same situation applies to the inlet at Njord Heim, actually a large pond literally dynamited out of the limestone to form a harbor. The channel is narrow, and there is apt to be considerable surge at the inlet in certain winds and seas. Njord Heim does offer the advantage, however, of constant vigilance at the marina's radio, and the marina operator, Els Ellefson, is most helpful in offering weather conditions, advice, and counsel.

More about the individual harbors and facilities for sailing/cruising on Green Bay in subsequent chapters. But suffice it to say at this point that it is beautiful cruising water with generally favorable weather and winds and a host of small ports where the visiting sailor will be greeted most cordially. It well could be called the West Channel.

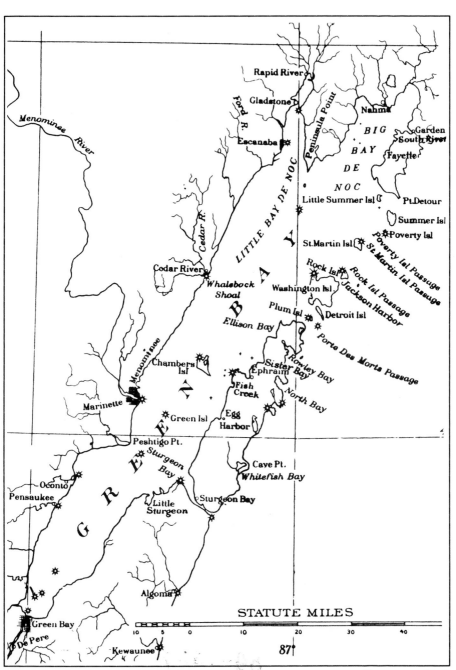

STATUTE MILES

10   5   0   10   20   30   40

87°

Summer Sail

2

THESE
HISTORIC WATERS

The yachtsmen cruising Green Bay should know that they are traversing historic waters, following in the wake of French *coureur de bois* who first visited this area 350 years ago.

In the historic search for a passage to the Orient, Jean Nicolet led a party of Indian canoeists into the waters of Green Bay in 1634. There followed in rather rapid succession additional French explorers, many of whom were missionaries; then the *coureur de bois* who came to trade for the Indians' furs.

Not surprisingly, these canoeists took a protected course from Canada to Green Bay, much as sailors do today. They followed the Ottawa River west from Montreal, thence took the Mattawa River into Lake Nippising. From there, it was a short portage into the French River which runs west again and empties into Georgian Bay. From there, they used the sheltered waters of the North Channel until they had to cross a piece of open water at the northwest end of Lake Huron, through the Straits of Mackinac, then along the north shore of Lake Michigan into Green Bay.

Nicolet got as far as the river which empties into Green Bay at its southern end, named the Fox River after the Indian tribe which occupied that area at the time.

Fr. Pierre Marquette took over where Nicolet left off and travelled the Fox River up its many swift rapids to Lake Winnebago, and thence through the upper Fox to where it comes within a mile of meeting the Wisconsin River. Portaging into the Wisconsin, Fr. Marquette followed its southwesterly course and discovered the Mississippi.

This water system became the prime route for exploration and then trade from this entire area back to French Canada, and it was along this route that the first settlers came and established trading posts, missions, then small settlements in the Green Bay area. As I mentioned above, these are historic waters, and an appreciation of the early history of this area will add to the yachtsmen's enjoyment of their Green Bay cruise.

Considerable mystery surrounds the origin of the name Green Bay. The earliest French charts of the area label it *La Baye de Puants* (also spelled *Puans*). The name came from the Winnebago Indians inhabiting the region who were called *Puants*. In the Indian language, this meant "stinking water." But there is no clear cut answer as to why that name was applied to the Indians or the bay. In later years, *La Baye de Puants* was shortened to *La Baye*, and the settlement at the mouth of the Fox River became *Fort La Baye*.

When the British took control of this area in the 1760s, they changed the name to Green Bay. It is thought the name came from the verdant foliage on the shores of the bay rather than from the color of its water. The earliest map showing the name Green Bay was published in 1769, and the name came to be applied to the settlement as well.

Weather broadcasts are available from the airport in Green Bay on weather channel one, but the signal begins to fade when you get up into the northern end of Green Bay. At that point, you can sometimes pick up the weather forecasts from Marquette, Michigan, which are of some value, and on W2 channel from Traverse City, Michigan. The latter, however, have to be interpolated for the west shore of Lake Michigan rather than the east. The forecasts are labelled "near shore" and are applicable only five miles from shore. They are usually followed by forecasts for the open waters of Lake Michigan.

You will need the following charts for navigation purposes in cruising Green Bay:

New Numbers	Old Numbers
14900	7
14902	70
14908	701
14909	702
14910	703
14918	725
14919	728

The magnetic declination was 2°, 30′ in 1981 and the annual increase is 9′. Loran grids are in the 32000 and 48000 series.

There are a number of commercial radio stations up and down the bay on both sides, most of which are aware that sailors use their broadcasts for information on weather conditions on the bay.

Marine radio telephone service is available on channel 87, connecting with a station of the Lorain Marine telephone service at Sturgeon Bay. This channel is easily contacted from anywhere on the bay.

Be sure to bring a dinghy for your Green Bay cruise, for there are numerous opportunities to anchor out and row ashore for nature walks, exploration, rock collecting, swimming, and even more important for those who are addicted to it, fishing.

Fishing for delicacies such as perch and smallmouth bass has always been good in Green Bay waters, along with walleyes in certain areas; but an explosion of large size trout and salmon in recent years offers some of the finest fishing for those species anywhere in the U.S. Perch and bass fishing can be found along any of the rock shores, generally right where the shore shelf drops off, as well as on the rock reefs off many of the islands. There has been considerable planting of walleyes in the Sturgeon Bay area, and both Big and Little Bay de Noc have long been noted for their walleye fishing.

Brown trout come into shallow waters each spring, soon

after the ice goes out, to feed on the large quantities of spawning smelt and are present in shallow water again in the early fall when the browns come in to spawn themselves. Somewhat the same is true of rainbow trout and large brook trout, but the prize of all are the chinook salmon which have been planted in recent years by the Wisconsin Department of Natural Resources.

Fishing for salmon is particularly good on the Lake Michigan shore from Algoma north to Baileys Harbor, including the Sturgeon Bay ship canal when they come to spawn in the fall. Good salmon fishing grounds are also found off the west shore of Washington Island and in most of the harbors along both shores of Green Bay. Licenses are needed in both Wisconsin and Michigan along with a trout stamp in Wisconsin. But short-term ones are available to out of state visitors.

Green Bay may not have tides like the ocean, but it does have have its own peculiar variety of mini-tides. They are called *seiches* (pronounced *SAY-shez*). These mini-tides produce water level changes of a foot or more every nine to eleven hours at the southern end of Green Bay, although one-inch changes are more typical in the northern bay and the rest of Lake Michigan. The seiches are caused by atmospheric disturbances: pressure changes and winds. Green Bay's long narrow shape and shallow depth concentrate these water level changes at its closed end near the city of Green Bay. The overall effect is like water sloshing back and forth in a bathtub.

The periodic fluctuations caused by the seiches should not be confused with the bay's long-term, year-to-year water level changes. The level of Green Bay is the same as that for other parts of the basin formed by Lake Michigan and Lake Huron and will vary considerably from one year to the next depending upon long-term weather conditions. Seiches are also distinct from ocean tides which are produced by the pull of the moon's gravity as it circles the earth.

On rare occasions, the seiches may result in rapid water level changes of several feet, particularly under the influence of strong northeast winds which pile up the waters of Green Bay at its narrow end. For the yachtsman, the presence of the seiches dictates leaving a reasonable amount of slack in dock lines when tying up to fixed piers.

There is an excellent section in the Great Lakes Cruising Club's guides about Green Bay cruising, and some of the basic information for this book has been obtained from that source.

The Wisconsin Division of Tourism has also published a book on Wisconsin harbors which is available from the Department of Natural Resources, Division of Tourism, P.O. Box 7970, Madison, WI 53707. The *Michigan Harbor Book* is also available through the Michigan Department of Natural Resources, P.O. Box 30028, Lansing, MI 48909.

I have utilized these reference materials in compiling this book, but I have also attempted to inject rather frequent personal observations from a number of years of cruising Green Bay waters. I hope that the book is not only valuable for you to plan your cruising but is also entertaining.

A SPECTACULAR INTRODUCTION. French explorer Jean Nicolet, in search of the elusive Northwest Passage, led the first expedition of Europeans into Green Bay in 1634. Nicolet had heard tales of rich Indian kingdom to the west, the land of the Puants. Instead, he found the Winnebagoes, descendants of the fabled Puants. The mural depicted here can be seen at the Neville Museum in Green Bay. *Courtesy Neville Museum*

SMITH QUARRY. Looking east from Sawyer Harbor, which is in the foreground, near Sturgeon Bay, the onlooker gets a spectacular view of Smith Quarry, one of several such operations that boomed in the 19th century. Exporting limestone to the mills of Milwaukee, Chicago, and Gary was a major industry all up and down the Door County Peninsula, and ships like the *J. T. Wing* pictured on page 25 did a thriving business hauling the soft rock to the southern ports of Lake Michigan. For the sightseer visiting Door County, the quarries are a must attraction. *Roy Lukes photo*

LAST OF THE SCHOONERS. This is the *J. T. Wing* with a full load of lumber aboard. The picture was taken in 1936. She was the last of the commercial sailing vessels to ply the Great Lakes, but thousands of her predecessors provided the principle means of transportation for many years before the arrival of the railroads and steam-powered craft. These ships carried everything from lumber to limestone to pig iron to markets in Milwaukee and Chicago, then brought back finished products from manufacturers in those cities to the ports along the upper reaches of Lake Michigan. It was not a business without risk, for the winds of the lake were often more than treacherous. Without modern weather forecasting available, many ships were sent to the bottom in fierce storms. *Courtesy of the Neville Museum, Green Bay*

RIVER BOAT LIVES AGAIN. Steam replaced sail on the Great Lakes, but not all at once. All sorts of craft from side-wheelers to stern-wheelers to screw-propelled ships plied the waters of Lake Michigan. But only paddleboats could navigate the rivers. The *River Queen* is a modern version of those stern-wheelers that carried passengers and freight up and down the Fox, Wisconsin, and Wolf Rivers in Wisconsin during the last century, before the coming of the railroads to isolated rural areas. A series of locks along the Fox and a canal connecting the Fox with the Wisconsin near Portage made it possible for a traveler to go all the way from Green Bay to New Orleans via river boat. This is no longer possible because several locks have been abandoned or removed, but riding on a river boat is still available. The *River Queen* takes sightseers on a trip on the Fox River, departing from DePere, just south of Green Bay, during the summer months. There is a cocktail cruise for those who are interested, and on occasion, a Dixieland band comes along to liven up the atmosphere. *Courtesy of Green Bay Visitors Bureau*

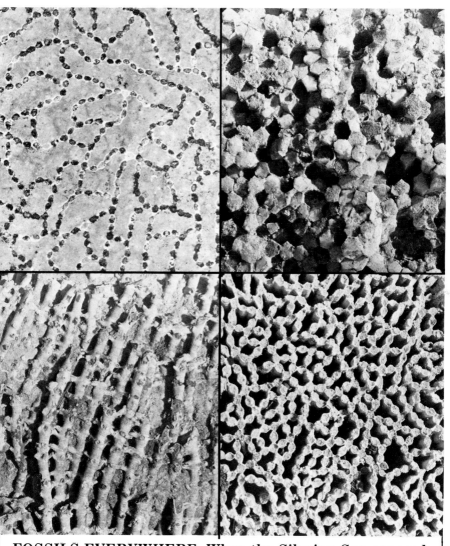

FOSSILS EVERYWHERE. When the Silurian Sea covered the Great Lakes area, the inland ocean teemed with billions of creatures, but all of them were left high and dry when the first Ice Age sucked up all the water and the earth's crust shifted, creating the Niagara Escarpment. Pictured here are chain coral, which can be found in abundance in Door County. *Roy Lukes photo*

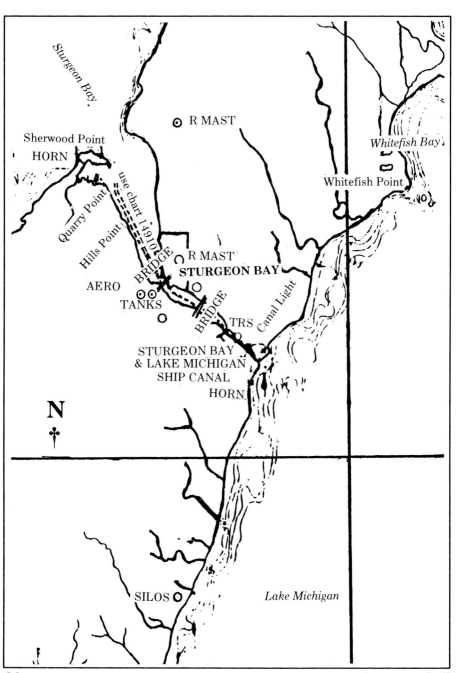

Summer Sail

3

STURGEON BAY
AND
SAWYER HARBOR

When the Sturgeon Bay ship canal was finally opened to marine traffic in the early 1880s, it was a boon to the sailing schooners which were at that time engaged in hauling lumber from the forests of northern Wisconsin and upper Michigan to southern Lake Michigan ports for the building of such cities as Chicago and Milwaukee. It is equally as important today for recreational boaters, providing an easy access from Lake Michigan to Green Bay and visa versa.

The canal cuts off 50 to 80 miles from a voyage from the west shore of Green Bay to Lake Michigan at the eastern entrance of the canal, depending upon whether the voyage originates in lower Green Bay, Marinette/ Menominee or Escanaba. By the same token, it cuts that much mileage off a voyage from Lake Michigan into Green Bay waters.

Digging the 7,400-foot canal was the lifelong dream of Joseph Harris who was the original publisher of the weekly newspaper in Sturgeon Bay, the Door County *Advocate*. He first suggested the formation of a construction company to dig the canal as early as 1860, and while his idea was originally greeted with skepticism as well as laughter, it attracted the attention of men who were vitally interested in the commercial development of the area; and in 1864 a state charter was granted to the Sturgeon Bay and Lake Michigan Canal and Harbor Company. Incorporators included the president of the Northwestern Railroad, northern Wisconsin's biggest lumber man, the Goodrich Transportation Company, and financial backers from as distant as New York City.

In 1866, Congress approved a bill granting 2,000 acres of land to the company with which to finance the construction. A large part of this land was in Marinette County on the west shore of Green Bay, and the arrangement was that the company could borrow against this timber acreage or sell it off to finance construction.

Even this financing proved insufficient to start the project, however, and curiously, it was the famous Peshtigo fire in the fall of 1871 that gave a final lift to the project, since Congress appropriated another $40,000 in disaster relief for the timber which had been burned on the company's land grant.

The first scoop of dirt was dug on July 8, 1872. The final two feet separating the waters of Lake Michigan and Green Bay were removed by two dredges working from opposite ends on June 28, 1878. The canal was then widened and deepened and commercial traffic began in 1880, although even then it was limited to light draft vessels or the larger craft in the lumber trade on their return trips. It was May of 1882 before the canal was officially opened for marine traffic.

The opening was celebrated with a six-day festival over the 4th of July that year, highlighted by a special edition of the *Advocate*. One of the pictures from the early *Advocate* shows a string of six lumber schooners being towed through the canal by a steam-powered tug.

The easy access to Lake Michigan and the other waters

of the Great Lakes became a principal factor in the development of Sturgeon Bay's large and noted ship-building industry. Boats of all sizes, from the smallest fishing tugs to 1,000-foot ore carriers, have been con-structed over the years by the three shipyards in Sturgeon Bay and of most interest to sailors are the custom yachts produced by Palmer Johnson which rank among the finest in the world. A number of boats built by Palmer Johnson in Sturgeon Bay have had notable careers in ocean as well as Great Lakes sail racing.

There is shoal water both north and south of the entrance to the Sturgeon Bay canal, so the shore should be given a wide berth of at least one mile. The canal light on a white tower built on land just north of the canal entrance is the aiming point by day or night. It is 107 feet above the water with visibility of 19 miles. Any ap-proaching course from 255° True clockwise to 350° True will clear all shoals. Head for the canal light, and when one mile off shore, enter the canal on course 314° True.

Approaching the canal from Green Bay, the only prob-lem is the extensive shoal off Sherwood Point, which is marked by a black lighted bell buoy with a black spar alongside. Skippers should not attempt to pass between this buoy and Sherwood Point without accurate local knowledge. The channel in Sturgeon Bay is well marked.

The Sherwood Point Lighthouse, incidentally, was built in 1883 and was originally lit by kerosene. When it was automated recently, it was the last manned light-house on the Great Lakes. The beam can be seen for 18 miles and the horn heard for 10 miles.

There are two bridges crossing Sturgeon Bay itself. The old bridge, called the Michigan Bridge, opens for pleasure craft on the half hour from 8:00 a.m. to 6:00 p.m. and on signal after that. The new high level bridge, called the Bayview Bridge, opens on signal, one long and one short. The center span height is approximately 50 feet.

Sturgeon Bay can well be called the boat capital of the entire area, not only for its extensive shipbuilding facilities, but for a number of excellent accommodations for pleasure craft which find the location particularly suitable since they have immediate access to Green Bay or Lake Michigan. A sizeable charter sport fishing fleet is also docked there.

Approaching from Lake Michigan, the first facility is Snug Harbor on the north side of the channel just west of the Bayview Bridge. This is operated by Palmer Johnson, and arrangements to stay there must be made through that office, telephone 1-414-743-4414. Ice, water, telephone, and fuel supply are available at the dock, and moorings are also available.

The Sturgeon Bay Yacht Club lies about one mile west of Snug Harbor on the opposite shore. The approach should be made in the channel until the club bears 238° True, then swing directly for the dock. Dockage is available, with complete facilities, water, ice, electricity, telephone; and the club has excellent shower and toilet facilities, a fine bar, and restaurant. Arrangements may be made to leave your yacht at the club for short or long stays.

Baudhuins, now Sturgeon Bay Yacht Harbor, adjoins the yacht club, and while it is principally a base for power boats, tie-ups are available for transient sailboats. Complete yacht services are available, including a well supplied marine store, hauling, electrical and mechanical service, and a good supply of lake charts. Not a bad place to stop on your initial visit cruising Green Bay. There is a travelift with 35 tons capacity, and many yachtsmen put their boats up for the winter there since sailboats can be stored with mast erect.

Palmer Johnson lies on the north side of the channel just east of the highway bridge and provides limited dockage. Again, a full inventory of marine services is available, along with water, telephone, supplies, ice, gas, and diesel fuel.

There is a relatively new marina, Port Door, between the old highway bridge and Bay Shipbuilding. And full services are available there.

Sailors may well want to take a look at the extensive shipbuilding facilities in Sturgeon Bay. At the noted

STURGEON BAY

(Wisconsin Division of Tourism photo)

Anchorage

Sturgeon Bay
Yacht Club

Baudhuin
Yacht
Harbor

N

The Moorings

SAWYER HARBOR
(*Wisconsin Division of Tourism photo*)

Palmer Johnson yards large custom yachts are usually under construction or being fitted out. Peterson Builders specializes in crafts such as mine sweepers for the U. S. Navy, tuna boats for the Pacific fishing trade, and ferries for the Alaskan service. At Sturgeon Bay Shipbuilding, you can observe the graving dock where lake carriers of up to 1,000 feet are assembled and repaired.

Sturgeon Bay is the retail shopping center for the Door County area, and all types of supplies are immediately available.

Yachtsmen wishing a quieter place to stay overnight in the area may wish to proceed northwest to Sawyer Harbor, just inside Sawyer Point at the entrance to Green Bay.

There is a gravel bar in the middle of the entrance to Sawyer Harbor which carries six feet at low water datum. To avoid any problem with this bar, hold to the ship's channel until the point of land on the port side hand bears about due west, then swing sharply 90° and bring the tip of the point well aboard on the starboard hand, giving it about two boat lengths leeway. There is good anchorage available just inside this point, or you may proceed on a course of 285° magnetic to the docks at The Moorings. Gas, ice, and food are available at what used to be called the Idlewild Pines Motel.

The Gitchie Gumee docks, marked by a private lighthouse, lie across Sawyer Harbor from the Moorings but are available only to crafts drawing less than four feet. The anchorage just inside the point is also an excellent spot for a mid-day swim and lunch.

Having traversed the ship canal and taken on a full compliment of stores in Sturgeon Bay, we are now ready to embark on our cruise of the beautiful Green Bay waters.

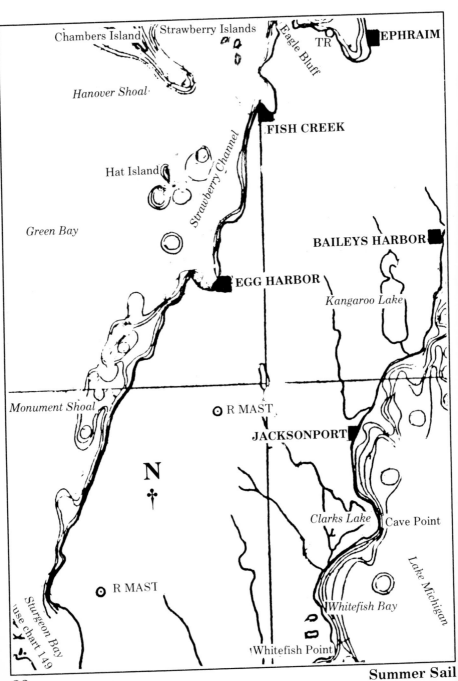

Chambers Island · Strawberry Islands · Eagle Bluff · TR · **EPHRAIM**

Hanover Shoal

FISH CREEK

Hat Island · Strawberry Channel · **BAILEYS HARBOR**

Green Bay · **EGG HARBOR** · *Kangaroo Lake*

Monument Shoal · ⊙ R MAST · **JACKSONPORT**

N

⊙ R MAST · *Clarks Lake* · Cave Point · *Lake Michigan*

Sturgeon Bay use chart 149 · *Whitefish Bay* · Whitefish Point

Summer Sail

4

A HARBOR
FULL OF EGGS

Egg Harbor is the first port of call north of Sturgeon Bay on the Door County side of Green Bay, and it is a delightful place for sailors to visit for a number of reasons. First, it is a deep bay with as much as 30 feet of water in the center, steep-to shores and a beautiful sand beach at the south end, and offers fine protection from almost any weather. It is one of the sailing meccas on Green Bay, affording fine facilities for the visiting skipper.

Curiously, the harbor did not get its name from its shape, but since the name Egg Harbor is such an unusual one, a dip into history is appropriate.

The newspaper of record in Door County, the *Advocate*, reported back in April of 1862 that the name derived from an expedition of a fur trader from Green Bay to Mackinac Island with the furs he had accumulated in a year's trading in the area. His fleet left the Fox River in Green Bay in June of 1825 well provisioned for the trip to Mackinac and arrived off the harbor now called Egg Harbor on the second day in early afternoon. The decision was made to go ashore for dinner, not unlike the decision made frequently by sailors today, but on the way into the harbor a race developed between the two leading sailing vessels which became more heated as they progressed into the harbor. It was tradition in those days that the commodore's vessel would be the first to land, but an upstart crew on an accompanying boat made a run for it at the entrance to the harbor, and receiving an order from the charterer to desist, the crew of the craft, as a signal of bravado, held up an old broom. This insult could not be accommodated by the commodore, so he ordered the mess baskets opened and a brisk discharge began, not of balls of fire but of eggs. The attack was soon returned in kind. The battle went on for some time, but at length the commodore triumphed and the refractory boat was obliged to fall back.

The story in the *Advocate* states that the battle was renewed upon landing. The boats and crews presented a rather unusual appearance, the inconvenience being increased by the fact that some of the missiles used by the belligerents were not of a very agreeable odor. The fun ended with the commodore having to wash his outer garments, and while so employed, some mischievous party threw his cap and coat into the lake. All enjoyed the sport and none more than the merry and jovial Canadian boat men.

The story of the sham battle at "Egg Harbor" spread among boat people, and it is believed that to this rude frollicking may be attributed the origin of the name of this village in Door County.

To this day, crews of sailing boats are enjoying the merriment and hospitality extended by the villagers in Egg Harbor.

There are no shoals to bother the visitor, and holding is good almost anywhere in the harbor. The primary overnight accommodation for transients is at a very fine marina constructed in recent years by the village.

A breakwater extends 450 feet in dog-leg fashion out from the east shore and is equipped with finger piers, the outer two of which are reserved for transients. The boaters who maintain their craft there on a summer-long basis are also frequently away on cruises, and the dockmaster is happy to accommodate transients in those slips. There is a mooring area established just east of the marina facility, and although the moorings are privately owned and maintained, there is room for a few boats to anchor in that area. There is also good holding to the south of the village dock in front of the Alpine Resort, which also has a small dock. That dock is 200 feet long and is generally occupied by boaters who rent spaces for the summer, but on occasion one or two boats can be accommodated there. Along the south shore of the harbor, there are a number of private docks, but they are not available to visiting sailors. The same is true of a very fine facility just inside the south point of Egg Harbor which again is privately owned and not available except in case of emergencies. The village dockmaster is equipped with marine radio and monitors channel 16 and will try his best generally to accommodate visitors. There is also a landing ramp for sailors who might wish to launch their boats from trailers to begin a cruise in that area.

The walk up the hill to downtown Egg Harbor is only a long block, and here the sailor will find a well provisioned grocery store, a hardware store which has an ample inventory, a service station on the main corner operated by the Mueller brothers, Herb and Bob, who are most accommodating and also service the gas pump on the dock. Water and pump-out are available, and ice can be gotten in the village. There is a small engine repair service available, operated by Dave Lautenbach, who generally answers sailors' emergency calls with dispatch.

In addition to this, there are ample facilities available for libations and dining, starting with the The Blue Iris Inn, formerly the Thimbleberry Inn and now run by Jack and Greg Janssen, on the main corner at the top of the hill. This fine restaurant has served the area well for over 100 years.

Just down the street on the opposite side is another restaurant, appropriately called Stage Station since that is where the stagecoach stopped in early days, Tony and Sara Demariness serve family style Italian food at reasonable prices. During the day, they also serve some of the finest hamburgers and cheeseburgers from a grill in the friendly bar.

Up the street is a well known watering place known as Casey's Inn, serving breakfast, lunch, and dinner. Bob Manson, the former chef at the C & C Club in Fish Creek, provides his customers with good food and a friendly atmosphere.

There is also the Villager, a restaurant that does not serve any alcoholic beverages. It's a fine place to enjoy breakfast and, on several nights a week, serves a well prepared fishboil. There is also a wonderful home bakery where croissants and other goodies are made fresh every morning.

The village maintains a public beach within walking distance of the marina that also includes a children's recreational park. There is a park area adjacent to the village dock with facilities for grilling out, picnic tables, and so forth. For boaters, there are toilet facilities but no showers.

The Alpine Resort boasts a 27-hole golf course and tennis courts which are open to the public on a fee basis. Showers are available at the golf course. For sailors who like to spend some time ashore in those pursuits, Egg Harbor is an excellent place to put into for several days.

Three miles inland at the Birch Creek music school students put on concerts in modern jazz and classical music several nights a week during July and August.

Most important of all, however, is the very friendly, hospitable attitude of the natives of Egg Harbor and also the members of the Egg Harbor Yacht Club whose headquarters is at the village dock. Any of the latter stand ready to share knowledge of cruising in the area with visiting yachtsmen.

Summer Sail

EGG HARBOR
(Wisconsin Division of Tourism photo)

Village Marina

Anchorage

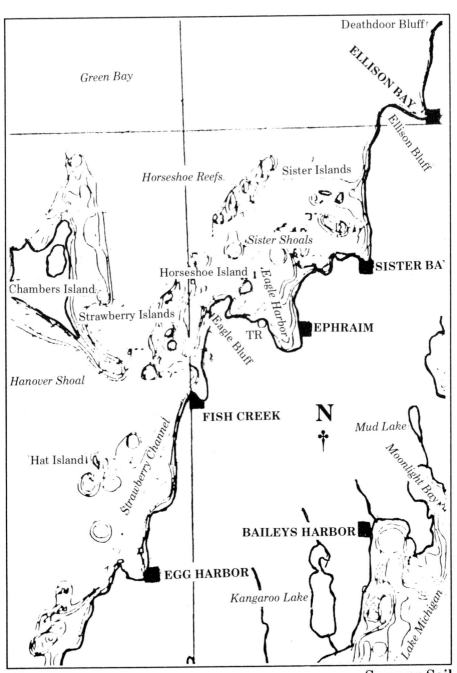

Deathdoor Bluff

Green Bay

ELLISON BAY

Ellison Bluff

Horseshoe Reefs. Sister Islands

Sister Shoals

SISTER BAY

Horseshoe Island

Eagle Harbor

Chambers Island

Strawberry Islands Eagle Bluff TR EPHRAIM

Hanover Shoal

FISH CREEK

N

Mud Lake

Hat Island

Strawberry Channel

Moonlight Bay

BAILEYS HARBOR

EGG HARBOR

Kangaroo Lake

Lake Michigan

Summer Sail

5

HARBORS
WET AND DRY

The next harbor north along the Door County shore is Fish Creek, the oldest resort area in the county and the site of Door County's first white settler, Increase Claflin. The harbor takes its name from a small creek of the same name and also from the fact that it was for a long time the principle fishing center of the Peninsula.

The approach to Fish Creek from the south poses no problems except for a shoal stretching out from the southwest point of the harbor. Giving this point 200 feet or so clearance insures a safe entrance. From the north, however, the R6 Bell Buoy marking the Strawberry Channel should be passed close by since there is shoal water west of this buoy.

Fish Creek harbor is open to the north and northwest, but there are two dock facilities that offer good protection.

The municipal dock is a cement pier offering quite a bit of dock space, but much of it is taken up by seasonal renters. It offers protection from any wind, although a surge may be felt behind it. There is at least 8 feet of water at low water datum along both sides of the dock, and yachtsmen are welcome.

Nearby Alibi Dock is privately owned by the Baudhuin

Yacht Harbor people from Sturgeon Bay, but yachtsmen are welcome. You can phone for reservations. There is also 8 feet or more of water on either side of this dock. The dock is equipped with electricity, water, pump-out, and gasoline, and there are showers and laundry facilities available on shore. There is good holding at anchor beyond these docks, and many boats are moored there.

One of the finer watering places and restaurants in the area is located just two blocks up the street from the dock. The C & C Club has a large bar, excellent dining room, and nightly entertainment. There's a grocery and general store across the street.

Fish Creek also offers some of the nicer shopping facilities in the county, principally a mall development called Founders Square and also a fine clothing store, Bundas Hutch. Founders Square burned to the ground in early 1984 but is being completely rebuilt.

One of the attractions in this resort community is the Peninsula Players, a summer stock company which has been offring live theatrical entertainment for some 50 years in Door County. The Players are happy to provide transportation from the dock to the playhouse. And in the month of August each year, the Peninsula Music Festival attracts symphony devotees from all over the Midwest.

Fish Creek is the southern entrance to Peninsula State Park, one of Wisconsin's larger public parks. It stretches along the bay shore all the way from Fish Creek to the next harbor at Ephraim. The park contains an 18-hole golf course, a number of fine camping areas, some beautiful sand beaches, and miles of hiking trails.

Fish Creek has developed a reputation as the fun village of the Peninsula, and though it has no organized yacht club, a group calling themselves the "Ghetto Yacht Club" gathers there from all over the territory every summer weekend for days and nights of fun.

If you and your crew prefer a more temperate environment, however, best proceed further north to the next large resort harbor at Ephraim. As its name suggests, it was founded by a religious group in the mid-18th century and has remained a dry area to this date. That may be its most praiseworthy trait, however, for the harbor itself is basically unsafe in many wind conditions.

There is a private marina on the north shore of the harbor in the village, but there are very few accommodations available for transient boats. The same is true next door at the Ephraim Yacht Club. There are tie-ups available at the public Anderson dock, but this is wide open to any wind from the northeast all the way around the compass to the southeast and is not recommended for an overnight stay. Much better to avail yourself of a very fine natural harbor out at Horseshoe Island, which sits in the middle of Eagle Harbor off Ephraim. This harbor offers protection in all winds, the only caution being that in the latter part of the summer it accumulates a large growth of weeds which can be troublesome when lifting anchor or even fouling your water cooling system.

Across from Horseshoe Island is a very fine harbor known as Shanty Bay or Nicolet Bay, also part of Peninsula State Park. There is an excellent sand beach and good holding at anchor off the shore. It is well protected from the west, south, and east but is open to the north and northwest, and caution is advised in anchoring there overnight if the weather forecast indicates strong north or northwest winds.

Ephraim is a beautiful village and will remind any visitor of its colonial background with many of its buildings being all white and of colonial vintage. There are some fine resort hotels and motels here, but the visitor is generally advised to go outside the village for dining purposes, the primary reason being the fact that the village is dry. The English Inn on the highway south of Ephraim is one of the best restaurants in the area.

Ephraim is the northern gateway to Peninsula State Park, and again the 18-hole golf course and all of the other facilities of the park are readily available, including a historic play staged in a natural amphitheater every evening. There is a fine art gallery right on the Anderson dock, the Hardy Gallery, maintained by the Peninsula Art Association, and just up half a block from the dock is the Anderson General Store which again has been preserved by the Peninsula Art Association. It is strictly a museum, however. Supplies are not easy to come by in Ephraim.

Many sailing craft are moored in the lower end of Eagle Harbor, but the transient is warned that these private moorings are well founded and that it is poor holding at anchor in that part of the harbor. The best advice is to anchor in the inlet at Horseshoe Island for overnight, with Shanty Bay being the next best choice except for strong winds from the north and northwest.

Ephraim Yacht Harbor

Ephraim Yacht Club

N

Anderson Dock

EPHRAIM

(*Wisconsin Division of Tourism photo*)

Anchorage

Public Dock

Alibi Dock

N

FISH CREEK
(*Wisconsin Division of Tourism photo*)

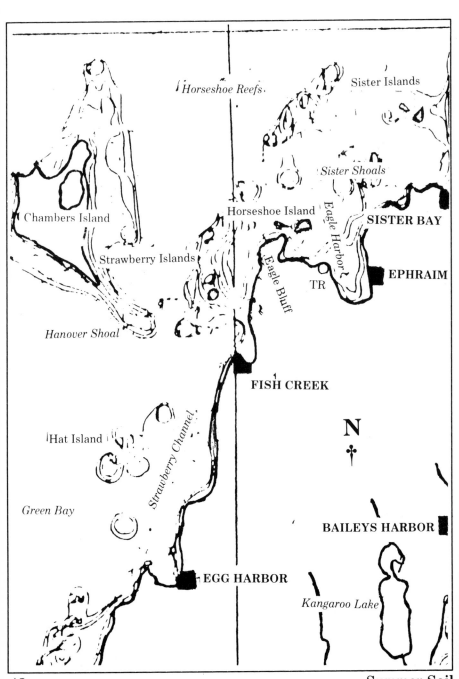

Horseshoe Reefs

Sister Islands

Chambers Island

Sister Shoals

Horseshoe Island

Eagle Harbor

SISTER BAY

Strawberry Islands

Eagle Bluff

TR

EPHRAIM

Hanover Shoal

FISH CREEK

Strawberry Channel

N

Hat Island

Green Bay

BAILEYS HARBOR

EGG HARBOR

Kangaroo Lake

6

ISLANDS
AND THEIR REEFS

A wine expert, so they say, is a person who drinks a lot of wine. That being true, the same applies to many aspects of sailing, where experience is the great teacher. I am, from that standpoint, an expert on the reefs in Green Bay waters, and I hope that I can pass on some of my knowledge so you can avoid that awful feeling when a sailboat goes aground.

The depth sounder is not always a reliable forecaster of trouble near the islands in Green Bay and their accompanying reefs. The glaciers which covered this entire area brought with them some huge granite boulders that they deposited in various places around the bay and which create veritable forests of underwater hazards.

At the end of the Silurian period in geological history, much of this region gently uplifted and the huge Silurian Sea began to recede. There followed a period of millions of years when the area was subjected to erosion, grinding off many of the prominent features. It was during this long period that plant and animal life began to proliferate in this area. This extensive interval lasted until what is known as the Pleistocene Period, better known as the Ice

Age.

The Pleistocene epic began about two million years ago and was featured by four major continental ice sheets which lumbered their way down from the Hudson Bay area. A number of changes in atmospheric conditions caused snowpacks to remain for long periods of years and to accumulate under the annual additions. The pressure created glacial ice which advanced on this area, creating major changes in its topography.

The great amount of water which was eventually tied up in these ice caps resulted in a dramatic lowering of the sea level to the point where it reached about 330 feet lower than it is today. Conversely, if the world's ice caps were to melt today, so much water would be released that the level of the oceans would rise about 200 feet.

The glacial lobe which effected the most changes in the topography of this area is only about 30,000 years old. Its icy tongues advanced from the Hudson Bay region into both the Green Bay and Lake Michigan basins. These advancing lobes did not skate along the land surface, they lumbered along, continuously incorporating local soil and bedrock within their bulk while leaving portions of their burden upon the landscape as deposits. These are grouped under the general term of glacial drift.

In eastern Wisconsin and particularly in Door County, there are numerous areas with concentrations of distinctive whale-shaped hills of till that were formed by the moving glacial ice. These streamlined, elongated mounds are called drumlins, and they rise up to 150 feet above the adjacent surface, extend up to two miles in length and typically are about one quarter mile wide.

These drumlins are plainly visible in many locations on the land surface of Door County, and they are also distributed over the bedrock of Green Bay, hidden by the waters. It is these underwater drumlins which form the islands and reefs of which the sailor must beware.

I once inadvertently became trapped in a forest of these huge boulders on the north shore of Hat Island. The youngsters sailing with me wanted to go for a swim and explore ashore. As the wind picked up from the south, the boat dragged anchor, and when I attempted to drop the anchor closer to shore, I ran dead on into one of these huge boulders although my depth sounder still registered 10 feet of water.

There is another similarly hazardous area just southwest of Hat Island known locally as Rock Awash. I have fished around this reef on a number of occasions, and the depth from the rocks which sometimes surface drops off to 20 to 25 feet just yards away.

All of this suggests a crew member on the bow with a lead line when attempting to anchor off any of the islands or reefs in Green Bay if stopping off for a swim or to fish.

There are a number of beautiful islands along the east shore of the bay extending from Egg Harbor to Ellison Bay, and a few of them provide excellent shelter for anchoring out for a swim and a picnic lunch, and a few have very nice beaches where you can put ashore. The reefs are generally an underwater extension of these islands.

The best one to visit is Chambers Island, the largest in the area. Chambers is over three miles long and a little less than two miles wide, and it contains a lake of its own in which there are two small islands. The lake, incidentally, is accessible from either the north or east shore and provides excellent fishing to anyone who wishes to tote a small dinghy ashore.

Chambers takes its name from an officer of a military expedition which was sent to the Green Bay area back in 1816 to establish the authority of the United States over what had previously been British territory. It was settled sometime before 1850 by a tall grisly Irishman named Dennis Rafferty, a fisherman. At the time, he was only resident of the area from Sturgeon Bay north except for Increase Claflin at Fish Creek. He was succeeded over the years by a number of other settlers who came there to cut off its pine forest, some of whom stayed as fishermen. At one time, it had a full array of town officers, its own school and post office, a sawmill and shipbuilding plant; all in all a well ordered community, which gradually fell in size after the island had been lumbered.

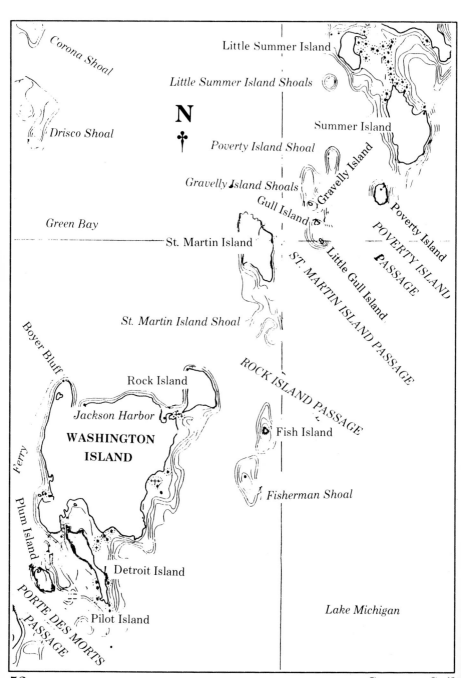

Corona Shoal

Little Summer Island

Little Summer Island Shoals

Poverty Island

N

Drisco Shoal

Summer Island

Poverty Island Shoal

Gravelly Island

Gravelly Island Shoals

Poverty Island

Green Bay

Gull Island

POVERTY ISLAND PASSAGE

St. Martin Island

Little Gull Island

ST. MARTIN ISLAND PASSAGE

St. Martin Island Shoal

Boyer Bluff

ROCK ISLAND PASSAGE

Rock Island

Jackson Harbor

Fish Island

WASHINGTON ISLAND

Ferry

Fisherman Shoal

Plum Island

Detroit Island

Lake Michigan

Pilot Island

PORTE DES MORTS PASSAGE

There was a considerable revival in its fortunes in the early part of the 20th century when Samuel Insull, the public utility magnate from Chicago, bought up much of the land on the island and began to convert it into an exclusive recreational estate, complete with golf course and airfield. That project went down the drain, however, in the Crash of 1929 and the subsequent Depression.

In more recent years, real estate developers have again been active on the island, and there are now quite a number of private summer homes on the shore around the 11-mile circumference. What was formerly a girls' camp is now owned by the Catholic Diocese of Green Bay, which has built a large retreat house there that is well used during the spring, summer, and fall months. The Diocese maintains a dock facility on the east shore of the island, but it is for the private use of people at the retreat house and the ferry boat, *Quo Vadis*, which carries people from Fish Creek to the island and back.

The most popular spot for a day's outing at Chambers Island is a large harbor at the north end which contains a very fine sand beach. There is good holding all around the island, however, and there are other fine anchorages available, depending upon the direction of the wind.

Given the normal southwest to westerly winds which prevail on Green Bay, another fine anchorage lies in the southern part of the east shore just north of and inside of Hanover Shoal. This is one of the reefs of which I write. It extends southeast from the southeast tip of the island over two miles out to a red spar. Charts show water of only one to two feet deep at low datum just inside of this spar, so yachtsmen are cautioned to proceed north past this spar before turning west into the shelter of the island.

There is also a long shoal extending due north from the northeast tip of the island, marked by a black bell buoy. And off the western shore another black bell buoy marks the western end of a reef off that corner of the island.

Given a north wind, there is good anchorage all along the south shore, although the beach here is gravel rather than sand.

Lying to the east of Chambers Island and off the Peninsula State Park shore is a series of four islands known as the Strawberries, starting with Big Strawberry on the south, then Little Strawberry, Jack Island, and Pirate Island. This is an area to avoid as it actually is one long reef with a few protuberances above water. As a matter of fact, the northern most island is under water most of the time. The islands are privately owned and not available for public use.

The reefs to avoid in the Strawberry Island area lie to the north and south of the islands. The north extremity of the reef is marked by a red nun. The southernmost point is marked by a black can which is about one mile due east of the red spar off the end of Hanover Shoal. This reef is known locally as Reimer's Reef since a number of yachts from the Marinette-Menominee area had to be hauled out at Reimer's Marina after going aground on their way home from the C & C Club in Fish Creek.

One of the most dangerous areas in this section of the bay is that surrounding Hat Island, a small rocky protuberance lying due north about three miles from Egg Harbor. It is a rookery for seagulls and terns, and a trip ashore is unpleasant except for botanists. There is a reef running due south from Hat Island about half a mile which ends at a point locally known as Rock Awash. This is a shallow pile of rocks which are sometimes exposed, but in any case not more than several feet under water. There is a red nun in the immediate area, but yachtsmen are cautioned that the can does not mark Rock Awash specifically but rather serves as the port side mark for boats entering the Strawberry Channel. The nun is actually about 300 yards due east of Rock Awash. There is also another shallow reef on the northeast corner of Hat Island.

Yachtsmen in Egg Harbor often use Hat Island as a mark on a racing course or just as a mark for a day's sail. It is safe to pass between the island and the aforementioned red nun, but anywhere south or southwest of the red nun helmsmen are cautioned to give Rock Awash a wide berth.

Yachtsmen proceeding either north or south along the

west shore of the Peninsula are cautioned to pass close to the R6 bell buoy marking the center of the Strawberry Channel. They should also proceed on a course of approximately 40° north or 220° south from Eagle Bluff in order to pass between Horseshoe Reef and the Sister Islands off the Sister Bay shore. Once north of the Sister Islands, there are no more water problems along the Door County shore.

I will deal with other reef problems as we proceed north on our cruise of Green Bay, although at this point I should mention Whaleback Shoal, a reef with only three feet of clearance at low water datum. It lies out in the center of Green Bay west from the Porte des Morts Passage. Whaleback Shoal is about seven miles off Deathdoor Bluff and is generally no hazard to boaters since most cruising courses will not take them near this shoal. It is marked by a red bell buoy at its eastern side and by a black spar on the northwest tip.

I won't attempt to advise sailors at this point on how to get off a reef after grounding, but I might add that there is an active Coast Guard Reserve available in Green Bay waters, particularly on weekends. There are also Coast Guard stations at Sturgeon Bay and Plum Island in the Porte des Morts Passage and rescue crews are available when there is danger to life or limb.

The best practice, however, is to avoid going aground in the first place, and I hope this chapter will help you avoid such trauma.

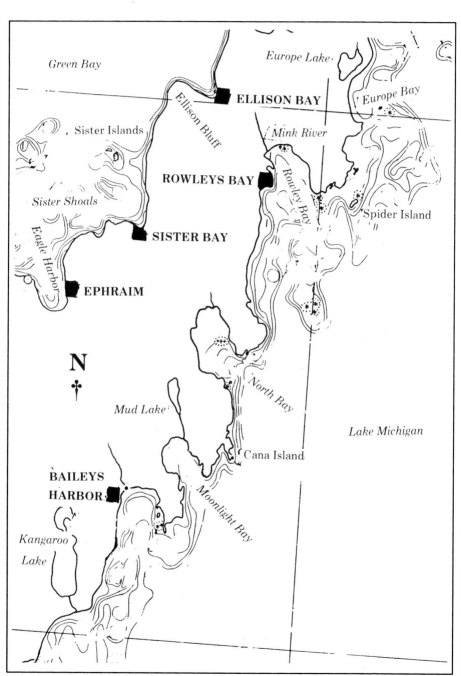

Green Bay

Europe Lake

ELLISON BAY

Ellison Bluff

Europe Bay

Sister Islands

Mink River

ROWLEYS BAY

Rowley Bay

Sister Shoals

Spider Island

Eagle Harbor

SISTER BAY

EPHRAIM

N

North Bay

Mud Lake

Lake Michigan

Cana Island

BAILEYS HARBOR

Moonlight Bay

Kangaroo Lake

7

SISTER BAY
A GOOD RESUPPLY
PORT

There are several good reasons for visiting Sister Bay, the next harbor north of Eagle Harbor and Ephraim.

One would be to visit Al Johnson's Swedish Restaurant, one of the most remarkable tourist attractions on the Peninsula. Sister Bay is the retail shopping center of northern Door County, and the Anchor Marina establishment of Fred Forkert is one of the better marinas on the Peninsula offering all types of marine service, including liftouts. There are sailboats of various sizes available for charter from Anchor Marina, if yachtsmen would like to start their Green Bay cruise from there.

Al Johnson's restaurant is authentically Swedish, including beautiful young blondes who come from Sweden each summer to work as waitresses in the restaurant or sales persons in the boutique. The roof of the building is covered with sod, and goats are tethered there to keep the grass mowed.

The village has constructed a fine pier and marina at a central point in the harbor, and it is within easy distance of Al

Johnson's and the shopping area. The steel breakwater is 300 feet long, and tie-ups are available on its lee side. There is also an additional dock inside the main structure which is 125 feet long and has finger piers for 22 boats. Water depths vary from 5 to 10 feet. Most of the slips are occupied by seasonal renters, but the dockmaster can usually accommodate transients. There is good holding and protection at anchor inside the breakwater. Gasoline, diesel fuel, ice, water, and pump-out are available at the village dock. Restrooms and showers are available in the village hall nearby.

Limited transient facilities are also available at Anchor Marina which is a fine all weather refuge harbor. The approach to this dock is from the south, inside of the mast, and minimum water depths inside are 6 feet. This is a complete service marina with haul-outs up to 38 feet. Mechanic personnel are on duty seven days a week. Gas, water, and ice are available at dockside, plus restrooms and a ship's store. It is also easy walking distance to Sister Bay's retail shopping area.

The latter includes a deli, bookstore, bakery, hardware store, drugstore, department store, supermarket, and even a bowling alley which also includes a very good restaurant, the Bay Bowl. There are a number of fine gift shops, notably Gage's, and a mile south on the highway is a new shopping center with several high-grade shops, including one handling gourmet foods.

Yachtsmen approaching Sister Bay from either north or south should stay close to shore where there is good water on either approach. The problem area is offshore, the two Sister Islands and the Sister Shoal. The islands are low-lying and barely visible under poor weather conditions. They are marked by two black cans which are difficult to find from any distance.

Sister Bay is a must stop on any Green Bay cruise, if only for lunch and window shopping.

SISTER BAY
(Wisconsin Division of Tourism photo)

N

Anchorage

Village
Dock

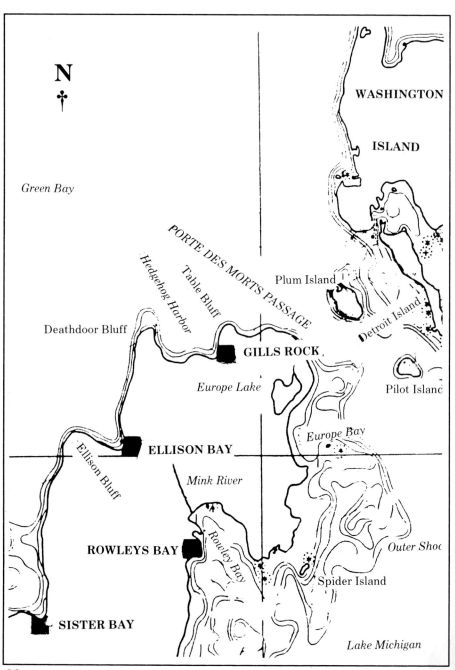

8

A CHARMING PICTURESQUE HARBOR

One of the most spectacular limestone bluffs in the entire 200 miles of Door County shoreline marks the entrance to Ellison Bay, one of the most charming harbors on Green Bay in my opinion. I always make it a point to spend at least one night there on any cruise of the bay.

The water off the bluff at the south entrance to the harbor drops off precipitously so that one can anchor within 50 feet of the shoreline and enjoy the swimming.

The only safe tie-up in the harbor is at the Cedar Grove Resort Marina where owner Herald Smith has invested many thousands of dollars in upgrading the facilities in recent years. He is an affable host and is usually waiting at the end of the dock to help you in. It is wise to contact Cedar Grove in advance by telephone (414-854-2006), and although they will not guarantee a reservation, they will usually tell you that they will be looking for you upon your arrival. They can be contacted on channel 16 as you near the harbor.

There are excellent dock facilities here, plus water and

electricity, a fine swimming beach, and picnic and outdoor cooking facilities. The docking fees are on the high side.

One of the charms of Ellison Bay is the small village itself which up to now is less commercially developed than most of the other resorts or villages on the Peninsula. Just two blocks up the road from the dock is a fascinating old general store where almost any type of supply is available including ice. On the other corner is the Viking Restaurant, featuring fine home-cooked food and one of the better fish boils on the Peninsula. The Viking does not serve liquors, not even beer or wine, but there are two fine supper clubs available up the road, the John Ellison Inn and Pub and the Hillside Restaurant.

Speaking of fish boils, these are a Door County tradition which have become a well publicized tourist attraction. The idea of boiled fish may not appeal to you at the outset, but be assured that this is gourmet dining. Small new potatoes with the skins on and sweet white onions are put into the boiling kettle first, the kettle being heated by a wood fire. When these are practically done, steaks of either whitefish or trout are put in to boil for an exact period of 12 minutes. Large quantities of salt, one pound for each five pounds of fish if you can believe that, are dumped in the water, the purpose being to keep the flesh of the fish firm during boiling. At the last moment, kerosene is thrown onto the fire to create a particularly hot blaze and the entire kettle boils over, spilling out any fish oil which may have accumulated on the surface. At this point, fish, potatoes, and onions are quickly removed and served topped with melted butter. It is a real feast.

The fish boil originated as a simple hot meal for fishermen who have worked the waters of Green Bay and Lake Michigan for whitefish and trout for many years. They put a pot of water on the head of their motor to heat, threw in potatoes and onions and pieces of the day's catch, thereby providing themselves with a hot meal at sea.

The public dock at Ellison Bay is available only to shoal draft boats. Overnight anchoring is also not recommended at Ellison Bay because the harbor is wide open to the north and west. If perchance no tie-ups are available at the Cedar Grove dock, the yachtsman is advised to proceed to Horseshoe Island to the south or to Washington Island to the north.

There is one other harbor on the Peninsula north of Ellison Bay: Hedgehog Harbor at Gills Rock. But there is very little here to offer cruising boats except that it is a handy spot to pick up passengers or drop them off since it is serviced by a bus line. This is one of the two docks servicing the ferry to Washington Island, but the rest of the docks in this harbor are used by the fishing fleet.

ELLISON BAY
(*Wisconsin Division of Tourism photo*)

Cedar Grove Resort

Town Dock

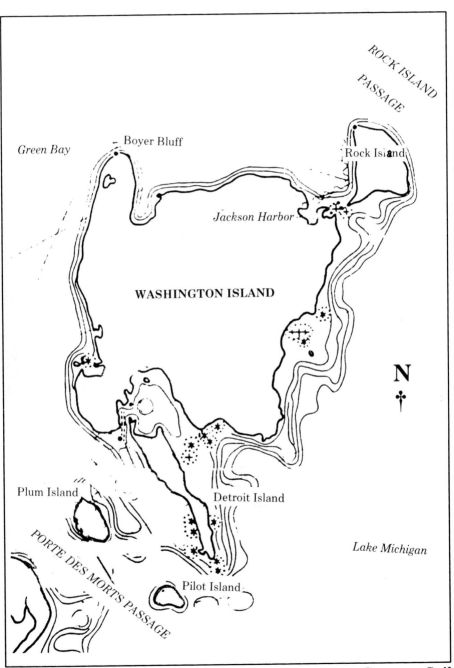

Green Bay

Boyer Bluff

ROCK ISLAND PASSAGE

Rock Island

Jackson Harbor

WASHINGTON ISLAND

N

Plum Island

Detroit Island

Lake Michigan

PORTE DES MORTS PASSAGE

Pilot Island

9

WASHINGTON ISLAND

No cruise on Green Bay would be complete without a visit to Washington Island, the pinnacle of beauty spots in the whole area. In fact, any such cruise should include at least several days on the island where there is a choice of four harbors.

Washington Island was occupied by a succession of Indian tribes long before the white man arrived in this area, for they too appreciated its great natural beauty, its natural air-conditioning from the winds and breezes that blow across it from both the lake and the bay, and some of the finest fishing in the area.

It was a battle for control of the island that gave the passage between the island and the mainland its name, Porte des Morts in French, Death's Door.

This area had long been occupied by various Algonquin tribes — the Ottawas, the Sacs, the Foxes, the Potowatomi, and the Menominees — all of whom had been driven westward by the warlike Iriquois. The Algonquins were primarily agricultural tribes living off the marvelous hunting and fishing and doing their own farming.

Then came the Winnebagoes, a branch of the Sioux,

who migrated into Wisconsin from the southwest. Extremely warlike people, the Winnebagoes started taking over more and more of the land of the Algonquin tribes, driving the Potowatomi further and further north up the Door County Peninsula until they were trapped on Washington Island.

Both tribes prepared for a climactic battle.

The Potowatomi, seeking to catch the Winnebagoes unaware, sent scouts by canoe to the mainland to locate a safe landing spot for their warriors, but the scouts were captured by the Winnebagoes who tortured them into revealing their tribe's war plans. They were to light a fire on the shore at a safe landing place so that their forces could cross by night and surprise the Winnebagoes, but the latter, alerted to the plan, lit such a fire on top of what is now known as Deathdoor Bluff. The Potowatomi crossed in their canoes but found themselves landing at the foot of a precipitous cliff where the waves soon demolished most of their canoes. A surviving few were able to escape to a ledge at the base of the cliff, and here a fight to the death with tomahawks ensued. The entire Potowatomi warrior force was wiped out, and as the story was handed down through the generations and ultimately to the French, that passage became Porte des Morts.

In later years when sailing ships carried all of the cargo and passengers from Mackinac Island to Green Bay and down into Lake Michigan, the reefs in the narrow passage took a heavy toll, adding to its reputation as Death's Door.

Today's sailors need to be somewhat cautious in traversing the passage because there are often two different winds, one from the bay and one from the lake, causing disturbed wave patterns and currents. The reefs are well marked, however, and normal caution will insure a safe passage.

There is no problem entering the Porte des Morts passage from the Green Bay side. The problem occurs on the Lake Michigan side. There are two shallow reefs which must be avoided.

The first is Waverly Shoal on the south side of the passage, marked by black bell buoy #5. Directly south of this is a black spar marking the outside of Nine Foot Shoal.

The other danger point is a shallow reef running west of south from Pilot Island. This shoal is not marked, and Pilot Island, which is the one bearing the lighthouse, must be given at least 2,000 feet of leeway to the south.

The course through the passage from Lake Michigan to Green Bay is 312° magnetic once the black bell buoy off Waverly Shoal is abeam on the port side.

Traversing the passage from Green Bay to Lake Michigan, the course is 132° magnetic until Waverly Shoal buoy is abeam on the starboard side, then a course of at least 120° magnetic out into the lake.

The other dangerous shoal to be avoided in this area extends southeast from the east end of Detroit Island. Sailors rounding Detroit Island and proceeding north must give the southeast tip of Detroit Island at least one-half mile berth.

There is also bad water between Detroit and Plum Islands, and there is no point attempting passage through that area. The best part of valor is to pass between Plum Island and the mainland even if heading for Detroit Harbor.

Washington Island has long been a haven for sailors going back as I have said to Indian times. The island got its name from that expedition dispatched by the United States after the War of 1812 to establish American sovereignty over the area and build a fort at Green Bay. One of the three schooners in the expedition, the *Washington*, was the first to arrive at the island, and the troops gave the name of their vessel to the harbor on the north side of the island and to the island itself. The island was first settled in the mid-19th century by a colony of Irishmen, but in 1870, W. F. Wickman, an Icelander, induced thousands of his countrymen to come to the U. S. and to settle on the island. To this day, Washington Island has the largest population of Icelandic people in the U. S.

Washington Harbor at the northwest corner of the

island was the center of all marine activity in those days of the sailing ships. The water there is very deep and offers good protection from all winds except from the north. Extensive docks and warehouses were erected there in those years, but they are long gone now, and only the underwater pilings remain.

There are no facilities in Washington Harbor today, but it does offer good holding at anchorage, particularly well down into the bay, and is prized by the gunkholing breed of sailors who value their privacy.

With the coming of the steamboat, marine traffic moved to Detroit Harbor on the southwest corner of the island. Detroit Harbor now serves as the island port for the ferries operated by Captain Arnie Richter. It is a busy harbor, and for that reason, the docks that are available are avoided by many transients. The ferry boat blows its whistle at 6:00 a.m. every morning to signal the first departing trip to the mainland.

For sailors who wish access to the shore, there is a well equipped dock maintained by Jim Anderson just beyond the ferry dock with 8 or more feet depth. Water and electricity are available here, and Anderson maintains a ship's store along with other sporting goods, such as fishing equipment just up the street from the dock.

Before getting to the ferry dock and just inside Lobdell's Point is Cap's Marina, which has 30 transient accommodations, electricity, water, showers, and restrooms and also a 30-ton marine travelift.

Sailors wishing more privacy should proceed into Peterson Bay, a beautifully protected harbor formed by Detroit Island to the south.

Proceeding up the marked channel in Detroit Harbor, leave the three red buoys, which mark the east side of the dredged channel, to starboard and turn to 065° true between buoys #6 and #8, leaving #8 close aboard to port. Hold this course until about 500 feet east of the spit of land that forms the west shore of Peterson Bay, then turn southward into the bay. Do not proceed much further east as there is a rock pile in the middle of the bay another 1500 feet east. There is from 7 to 10 feet of water available in this area at low water datum, and there is good holding. The passage to the east out of Peterson Bay is not navigable. (See the inset in chart #14909 of Detroit Harbor.)

There is another marina available in Peterson Bay, Hank's Island Marine. Here, gas, electricity, water, and restrooms are available, plus repair facilities and an 8-ton travelift and 15-ton crane.

No visit to Washington Island is complete without a tour of the island in Vi's taxi cab. There is a telephone immediately available on the dock at Detroit Harbor, and Vi can be summoned by radio telephone to her cab. She is a delightful person who was born and raised on the island and will give you its colorful history while taking you on a tour.

One unusual local custom needs mentioning at this point. During the Prohibition Era, islanders discovered that a concoction, namely Angostura Bitters, available at any grocery store, contained 45% alcohol. The natives started drinking Bitters straight with whatever was available for a wash. To this day, visitors are given a signed card certifying that they have had a shot of the local drink.

There are several good restaurants available on the island, specializing in the fresh whitefish caught just off its shores. Excellent fishing for bass and perch, plus trout and salmon, is also available.

Vi will also take you to the island museum and to the island art center. One of the local artists, Ray Breisemeister, who is in his 80s, has acquired a considerable regional reputation.

For those who would like to prepare fresh whitefish aboard, it is readily available, but visitors are cautioned that most of the fresh fish caught that day are iced down and shipped to the mainland on the 4:00 p.m. ferry. So shopping for fresh fish should be done by early afternoon.

One of the real delicacies available from the fishing boats are whitefish livers, which will put the ordinary chicken liver to shame. They are sweet and tender and need only a coating of flour before being quickly braised

DETROIT HARBOR
(Harmann photo)

N

Island
Outpost

Ferry
Dock

Kap's
Marina

KAP'S MARINA
(*Wisconsin Division of Tourism photo*)

N

NJORD HEIM

(Harmann photo)

Anchorage

in butter. Most of the fishermen part with their whitefish livers reluctantly, since they save them for their own enjoyment and their friends. It is a good practice to send your first mate dressed in her most alluring bikini to shop for whitefish aboard the fishing boats, and she should use all her charms to entice the fishermen to part with some of the livers.

A privately operated marina, Njord Heim, is available at the southeast corner of the island. The facility was constructed for members and property owners in the real estate development in that area, but it is available to the public. Reservations are suggested either by telephone (414-847-2011) or marine radio. The radio is manned from 8:00 a.m. until 10:00 p.m. The man in charge is Eldred Ellefson, and he is a most friendly fellow.

The Njord Heim Marina is guarded on the east by a long concrete capped breakwater, upon which are flown the four flags of Scandinavia along with the U. S. flag. These 30-foot poles mounted on a 15-foot high breakwater can be seen at a distance of up to 30 miles, depending on visibility.

There is a red nun located on the southwest corner of this breakwater. Care should be taken in aligning your entrance relative to the entrance buoy and the western point of the entrance channel since there may be considerable swell passing the end of the breakwater in a westerly direction.

Transient spaces are available at finger piers here, and there is electricity, water, showers, restrooms, pump-out, and fuel.

Njord Heim is an excellent jumping off spot for skippers planning to cross Lake Michigan, and it is also an excellent first stopping point after crossing the lake bound for Green Bay.

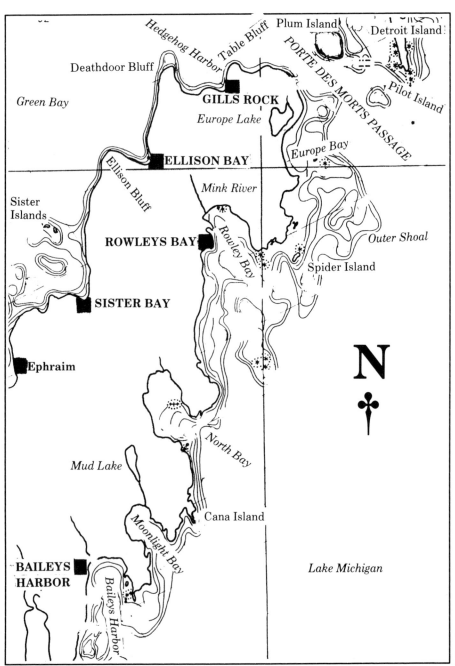

Green Bay

Hedgehog Harbor
Table Bluff
Plum Island
Detroit Island
Deathdoor Bluff
PORTE DES MORTS PASSAGE
Pilot Island
GILLS ROCK
Europe Lake
Europe Bay
ELLISON BAY
Ellison Bluff
Mink River
Sister Islands
ROWLEYS BAY
Rowley Bay
Outer Shoal
Spider Island
SISTER BAY

N

Ephraim

North Bay

Mud Lake

Cana Island

Moonlight Bay

BAILEYS HARBOR

Baileys Harbor

Lake Michigan

10

THE LAKE MICHIGAN SHORE

Visiting sailors may wish to take a side trip down the Lake Michigan shore to visit some of the ports on that side of the Door County Peninsula, the main one being Baileys Harbor. This is approximately 20 miles south along the lake shore from the Death's Door Passage.

There are two shallow harbors between the tip of the Peninsula and Baileys Harbor, notably Rowley's Bay and North Bay.

The Wagon Trail Resort in Rowley's Bay can accommodate transients up to 6 feet in draft and provide gas, electricity, water, showers, and restrooms. It is a full service resort with restaurant, indoor pool, tennis courts, and so forth, including boat rental and bait and tackle for fishing in the Mink River, one of the better known fishing spots in Door County. It is also easily accessible by dinghy.

The extensive shoals between Death's Door and Rowley's Bay all along that shore of Lake Michigan must be noted, however, starting with the outer shoal about

4 miles south of Pilot Island; the Nine Foot Shoal another 3 miles south; and finally Four Foot Shoal at the entrance to Rowley's Bay. These are all marked by red nuns.

Entrance to Rowley's Bay must be made from the south inside of red nun #8 off Four Foot Shoal. Red nun #2 and then #4 mark the east side edge of the channel, and a black stake #3 marks the west side. The Wagon Trail dock is on the port side, well up into the bay.

I personally would not recommend attempting an entrance into North Bay, which is the next bay to the south, despite the fact that there is a very nice resort there. Gordon Lodge has a fine dining room and cocktail lounge. This is a shoal harbor and submerged fish net stakes make it even more undesirable.

Baileys Harbor, however, provides excellent protection in all winds, and the Baileys Harbor Yacht Club is a fine place to spend a day or so. This is not a yacht club in the strict sense of the term but rather a public facility. It is an excellent resort. It has one of the finer dining rooms and bar in Door County, luxurious cottages, and in recent years a development of private condominiums.

There is an interesting story about how the Yacht Club came into being.

A wealthy Chicago attorney had two chief complaints about his summer stays in Door County. One, that there were no adequate facilities for his large cabin cruiser; and two, there wasn't any restaurant where he could take his wife to dinner wearing her mink stole and white gloves. He decided that he would build and operate such a facility.

Tragically, his wife was fatally injured in an automobile accident in England the spring that the resort was well under construction. He went ahead and finished it in her memory, however, and his Baileys Harbor Yacht Club provides a very fine marina and a top notch restaurant. It has changed ownership since that time, but the quality of the facilities and service has been maintained.

Full services are available at the Yacht Club dock, including gas and diesel fuel, electricity, water, showers, restrooms, and pump-out, and an attendant is on duty during all normal working hours.

Entrance to the harbor is marked by a black and white bell buoy well out in the harbor entrance, and then red and black nuns numbered 2 and 3 at the harbor entrance. There is a range light on shore that leads you directly into the harbor, and once well inside the harbor, Baileys Harbor Yacht Club facilities are on the starboard side. There is a flashing red light on an 8-foot mast at the entrance to the marina.

Some of the finest fishing in the area is to be found in Baileys Harbor: bass and perch, and more important, trout and salmon. There is excellent fishing at certain times of the year right off the Yacht Club docks.

A must visit for anyone putting in at Baileys Harbor is the Ridges Sanctuary nearby, a very unique series of ridges and bogs representing various stages in the level of Lake Michigan over the centuries. It has been preserved through private efforts and investment. Walking tours are available, including even a narrated tour for the blind. Over 100 varieties of native orchids can be seen here at various times in their blooming seasons.

There are also excellent shopping opportunities in the village of Baileys Harbor, along with a number of good restaurants. The Maxwellton Braes Resort, including a beautiful 18-hole golf course, is also situated just south of Baileys Harbor.

Baileys Harbor then is worth the side trip from Green Bay down into Lake Michigan and is also worth a stay of several days if the visitor has the time.

Summer Sail

N

Baileys Harbor
Yacht Club

BAILEYS HARBOR
(Wisconsin Division of Tourism photo)

ROWLEYS BAY
(*Wisconsin Division of Tourism photo*)

Wagon Trail Resort

N

JACKSON HARBOR
(Wisconsin Division of Tourism photo)

Anchorage

Public
Dock

Ferry
Dock

N

11

PICTURESQUE JACKSON HARBOR AND ROCK ISLAND

The most primitive, and therefore the most pictur-esque, harbor on Washington Island is at the northeast corner. Jackson Harbor is a relatively small, shallow har-bor, but it offers excellent protection from all winds.

It can only be approached from the west. Boats ap-proaching from Lake Michigan must round Rock Island to the north and come in from the western approach.

The entrance to the 90-foot channel is marked by a red tower atop a rock pile on the west and a black nun on the east. Give the red spar plenty of room and enter halfway between the red and black markers. At this point, aim directly for the nearest corner of the town dock. Hold this course until arrival at the dock. There is a black can just short of the dock which must be left to port and do not venture very far off the face of the dock.

The town dock is the only suitable tie-up point in the harbor; the other smaller docks being reserved for fishing boats.

Jackson Harbor has become very popular with transient sailors in recent years, creating a severe competition for dock space, particularly on weekends. And while friendly Jim Cornell will come around to collect the dockage fees, there is no radio communication available, so it is a matter of first come first served. Most sailors already tied up there are usually happy to be of help, however, and rafting can be expected.

Facilities at Jackson Harbor are also rather primitive. There is electricity and fuel available, and there are toilet facilities up the road a piece.

Jackson Harbor's charm, however, results to some extent from this lack of facilities. There is a nature preserve nearby offering an enchanting walk and a nice sand beach. The main fishing fleet on Washington Island also docks here, and fresh whitefish, and possibly livers, are available right on the boats. The day's catch is shipped out by mid-afternoon, however, so arrival by early afternoon is suggested if you want fresh whitefish for dinner.

There is telephone service at the dock, and Vi's taxi can be called to take you to the grocery store or for ice. None of these are immediately available at the dock. Jackson Harbor is also one terminus of the ferry serving Rock Island, a half mile away to the north.

Rock Island is a Wisconsin state park, and no vehicles are permitted. It is a wonderful natural environment for hikers, tenters, and swimmers.

There are limited spaces for transient boaters at the dock on Rock Island which services the ferry. Dominating the dock area is a beautiful stone boathouse of Icelandic architecture, containing on its upper floor a huge hall, the east end of which is dominated by a massive fireplace with an opening so wide an entire boat crew can stand inside. The building was erected by Chester Thordarson, a Chicago inventor and pioneer in transformer technology, who bought the island in 1910. In his great hall, Mr. Thordarson maintained the largest private library of Icelandic writings in the U. S. and also had a fine library of Audubon paintings. The library was removed to the University of Wisconsin in Madison in 1946, and the state, after purchasing Rock Island as a state park, has converted the hall into a recreation center featuring educational displays relevant to the plant and animal life on the island.

Not having been lumbered since 1910, the virgin birch, maple, and beech trees create a wildlife paradise. Forest birds and deer are abundant. And while most of the shore line is rocky bluffs, some of which rise almost 200 feet above the lake, the east shore has an excellent half mile sand beach. On the north point is Potowatomi Lighthouse built in 1837, the oldest lighthouse on Lake Michigan. In the days when commerce in this area was entirely waterborne, first by freighter canoes, then by sailing ships, Rock Island was the dividing point between those proceeding down the big lake to the immature ports of Milwaukee and Chicago and the more important route down Green Bay to the Fox and Wisconsin Rivers and the Mississippi, all the way to New Orleans.

The entire island is easily walkable over foot paths. There are picnic facilities, toilets, and campsites. The usual rules prevail, and the daily visiting fee is $2. Because of the limited number of boat spaces available, yachtsmen might be wise to leave their craft in Jackson Harbor and take the ferry over to Rock Island.

Summer Sail 83

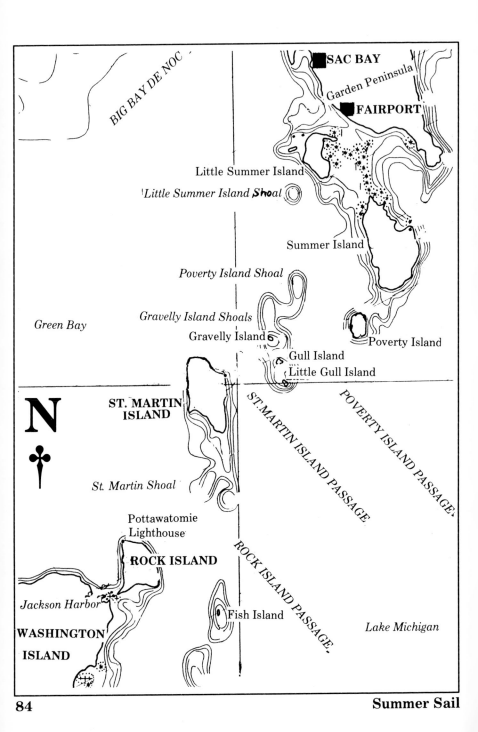

12

UP
THE ISLAND
CHAIN

The next island in the chain reaching from the Door County Peninsula in Wisconsin to the Garden Peninsula in Michigan is St. Martin Island, the home of a prosperous fishing colony in the mid-19th century. A community of several hundred people lived on the island in the 1840s and 1850s. They were attracted by the fine fishing in the waters around the island. The fish were salted down, packed in barrels, and shipped by schooner to Chicago, Milwaukee, and other lake ports.

The fishing industry also made the occupation of cooper a necessity to the island, for it was the cooper who made the casks into which the fish were packed and shipped. The casks were made by hand from wood available on the island.

The fishing business gradually petered out in the early part of this century, and all that remains of the habitation on the island are the stone foundations of the homes. Until recently, there was a manned lighthouse on the north end of the island, and the four Coast Guardsmen who were on duty there during the summer months were the only inhabitants of the island. But now they too are gone, and the island rests quietly with its memories.

There is no good overnight anchorage off St. Martin Island. The choices are between a shallow cove on the northeast tip near the lighthouse and a similarly shallow harbor on the south end. Both are adequate given the right winds, but both are highly exposed given a wind switch.

St. Martin Island is recommended rather for a daytime visit.

The same is true of Big Summer Island, the largest one at the north end of the island chain. Little Summer Island nearby is to be avoided because it is surrounded by shallow water. Big Summer Island itself, however, has a beautiful cove on its northeast side which affords a good anchorage sheltered from all but northeast winds. To enter the harbor, pick up the flashing white light on the northeastern point of Big Summer Island. Hold at least 400 yards off the point until the harbor is opened sufficiently to swing to a course of 224°. This will carry you into the center of the opening of the harbor.

For good holding in the harbor, look for areas of white sand devoid of weeds. It is a beautiful island to explore. There is an abandoned quarry and remains of a railroad running to the quarry from the shore. Years ago three old ships were sunk in a line to form a shelter and a dock from which the quarry stone was shipped.

There are some navigational cautions in this area. Do not attempt a crossing between Big and Little Summer Islands. The crossing between Little Summer Island and the mainland at Fairport require local knowledge.

Sailors proceeding north up the west side of the Garden Peninsula or proceeding northeast to Manistique are advised to make the passage south of Summer Island.

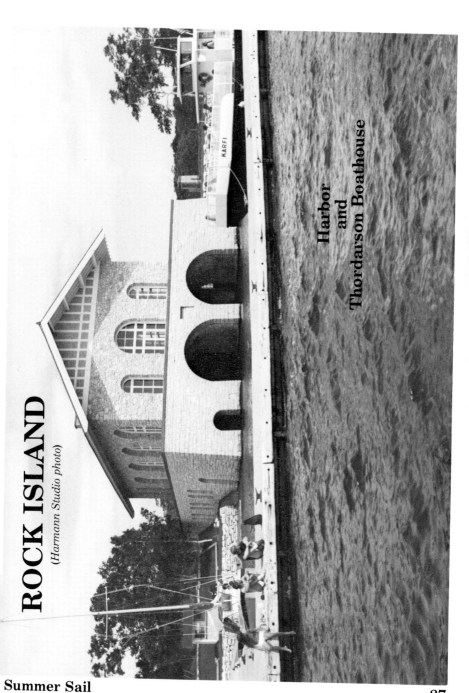

ROCK ISLAND
(Harmann Studio photo)

Harbor
and
Thordarson Boathouse

Summer Sail

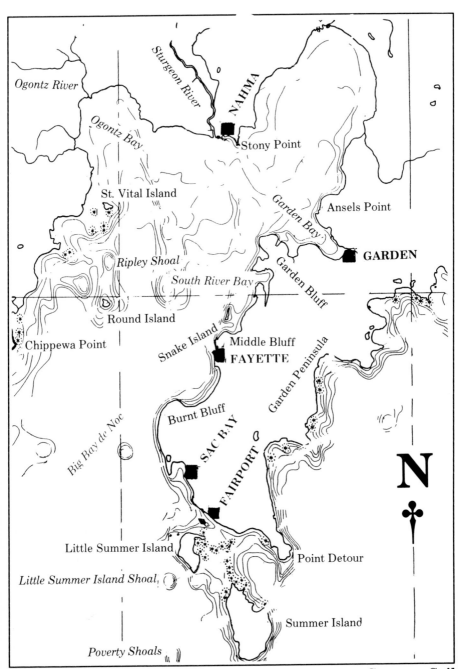

Ogontz River

Sturgeon River

NAHMA

Ogontz Bay

Stony Point

St. Vital Island

Garden Bay

Ansels Point

Ripley Shoal

GARDEN

South River Bay

Garden Bluff

Round Island

Snake Island

Middle Bluff

Chippewa Point

FAYETTE

Garden Peninsula

Burnt Bluff

Big Bay de Noc

SAC BAY

FAIRPORT

N

Little Summer Island

Point Detour

Little Summer Island Shoal

Summer Island

Poverty Shoals

Summer Sail

13

EXPLORING
BIG BAY DE NOC

There are four delightful harbors to visit on the west shore of the Garden Peninsula in Big Bay de Noc. The name, incidentally, comes from the Noquet Indians, a sub-tribe of the Chippewa who once inhabited the area.

Forget both Fairport and Sac Bay at the southern tip of the peninsula, but next consider a delightful stop-over at Burnt Bluff. This is a wholly man-made shelter, the work of Captain John Roen of Sturgeon Bay. It was maintained by his heirs until it was sold in late 1983 to a young entrepreneur, Tim Minahan, who plans further development there as a summer sailing resort.

A well protected breakwater parallel to the shore forms the marina, which offers spaces to transient boats. The entrance to the harbor is from north and is a bit difficult to recognize from any distance. There is an easily visible quarry on the shore which will serve as a marker. Look for a group of buildings just north of the quarry. The harbor entrance is just north of the buildings.

The harbor is small, so prepare all lines and fenders before entering. Head directly toward shore just north of the breakwater and turn into the harbor when the entrance is abeam. Hug the left side of the harbor entrance, for a gravel shoal sometimes builds up on the starboard side. There is good water depths at the docks.

Water and electricity are available at the dock and toilets and showers are available on shore. There are also both outdoor and indoor facilities for picnicking.

There are interesting spots to explore ashore, including the old quarry, which has Indian paintings on some of the walls, and several spectacular lookouts on top of the bluff. Wild raspberries are ample in season.

Tim monitors channel 16 and would be happy to welcome you ashore.

Four miles further north is the very unusual snail-shaped harbor at Fayette, a historic place in itself. This perfectly land-locked harbor was once a community of 1,000 souls and the site of an iron ore smelting operation which attracted many sailing schooners to bring in the ore and carry out the pig iron. The availability of limestone and hardwood made it an ideal spot for iron ore smelting in those early days, but the exhaustion of the wood supply did the operation in some 60 years ago.

Fayette harbor is now part of a state park, and the old charcoal furnaces and smelting towers have been restored by the state of Michigan so that visitors can recapture the glamour of the old roaring sailing schooner days which made Fayette a metropolis of the area at the time.

The harbor entrance is well marked by a flashing light. Pass this on the starboard hand, and when the harbor opens, sail in parallel to the high limestone cliffs. The water is deep along the shore.

The docks are in poor condition, but there is plenty of water. It is a matter of tying up wherever space is available. Anchorage is also available, but a caution about the heavy seaweed growth is in order at this point. By mid-summer, particularly when the weather has been unusually warm, seaweed growth becomes very heavy and thick in many of the harbors in Green Bay waters. Fayette is a good example.

The seaweed makes it difficult to get good holding. It also is a real hazard if you do not lift anchor from directly above. Dragging it any distance through the water will accumulate a load of seaweed which will make it very difficult to lift above water.

There are few facilities in Fayette. No electricity and no water at the dock, although there is a hand pump available a short distance away, and there are toilet facilities at the park. There are groceries, ice, and other supplies available in the nearby town, and they will deliver. The phone numbers are 644-2417 and 644-9213. Pay phones are available in the park. There is also a small restaurant and tavern about a mile south from the harbor. The first half of the walk is through the camping area; second half on blacktop country roads, an ideal hike after an excellent fish and chips dinner at the tavern.

The Michigan Department of Natural Resources is planning to build new docking facilities in Fayette Harbor and hopes to have them completed before the end of the 1984 boating season.

There are two very fine anchorages available just a short distance north of Fayette, in case the Fayette harbor is crowded as it sometimes is. One is an excellent anchorage between Snake Island and the mainland, offering good protection from all directions except north. Drop your hook in about 7 to 8 feet of water midway between the mainland shore and the small spit that marks the eastern shoal off the island. The bottom is sand and mud but good holding. Four miles north of Fayette is a beautiful, secluded, unspoiled anchorage in South River Bay, affording good shelter from all winds. Approaching from the south, a tangent from one-half mile off Snake Island to the tip of Garden Bluff will clear all offshore shoals. The entrance to South River is free of danger, but there are no navigational aids. Once in the harbor, proceed into the southerly arm where there are water depths of 10-12 feet. The anchorage in South River Bay is protected from all winds, but it has no facilities of any kind.

At the north end of Big Bay de Noc is Garden Bay, the largest bay on the east shore. Van's Harbor is the port of

Garden and lies approximately in the middle of the north shore of Garden Bay. The village of Garden is about a mile to the southeast and is only available by dinghy.

There are no really good tie-up facilities in Garden, and it is not a good anchorage, so the only purpose of a visit would be for supplies.

A tie-up with permission is available at the dock of the Big Bay de Noc Fisheries. Permission to tie-up should be sought from Mr. Hermis who owns the fisheries. Gas, diesel, fuel, water, and ice are available at the dock, and there is a good IGA store in the village.

The same tangent from Burnt Bluff to Garden Bluff will bring you opposite the harbor entrance, where a course of 127° will take you into the bay.

If you are not desperate for any supplies at this point, I would advise skipping Garden as a port of call and proceed west into Little Bay de Noc and up to the very delightful harbors at Escanaba and Gladstone.

MODERN RUINS. Fayette was once a thriving community. Now it is a state park. *Robert McCoy photo*

Summer Sa

BURNT BLUFF. This little harbor on the Garden Peninsula of Upper Michigan is run by Tim Minahan who purchased it in 1983 from the heirs of Capt. John Roen from Sturgeon Bay.

George Verheyden photo

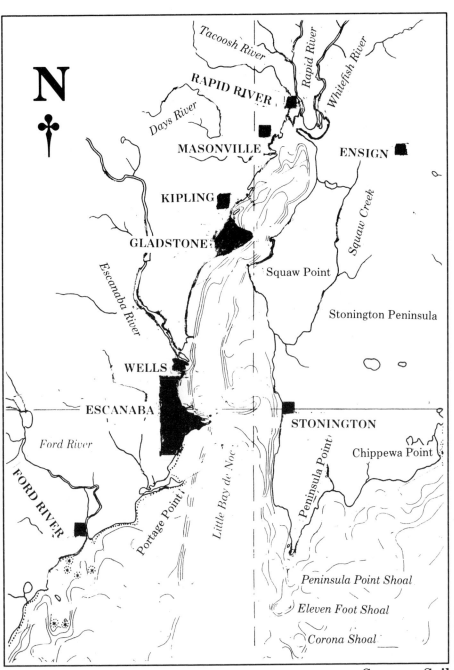

14

THE BAY'S
WESTERN SHORE

There are two major differences between the Michigan or west shore of Green Bay and the east shore along Door County and Garden Peninsulas.

In the first place, the west shore is low-lying and sandy, and there is a considerable area of shoal water off shore along the entire length of the bay, with shoals extending considerably off shore in some areas. These are actually glacial lake deposits.

The other major difference is in the quality of the harbors and marina facilities. Some years ago the state of Michigan segregated the tax on gasoline sold to boaters into a special fund which was used to build and maintain harbor facilities. The result is an excellence in quality of facilities available along the Michigan shore in contrast generally to the Wisconsin shore. This becomes immediately evident at both Escanaba and Gladstone in Little Bay de Noc.

Chart #14908 graphically depicts the shoal water along this shore in Little Bay de Noc. Boats approaching from the south have a straight run at the channel between the flashing black bell buoy off Ford River and the flashing red bell buoy off the southern end of Peninsula Point.

Crossing from the Garden Peninsula to the east, in other words an east to west crossing, there is good water between the R4 red bell buoy and the tower-mounted beacon at Minneapolis Shoal, although local knowledge is required to cross between the R4 bell buoy and Peninsula Point itself.

The red bell buoy marking the mid-channel just southeast of Escanaba should also be noted and should be passed close at hand.

The entrance to the marina at Escanaba is well marked, but the approach should be made due north until abeam of the flashing light at the mouth of the harbor. Hold to the north side of the entrance channel where 10 feet of water is found all the way into the yacht dock.

The dockmaster is on duty from 8:00 a.m. until 10:00 p.m. and will assist with tie-ups and assignment of overnight space. All the necessary facilities are available here: water, electricity, pump-out, marine supplies, and ice, plus excellent toilets and showers. A marine railroad and small boat hoist are also available. The marina adjoins a city park and swimming beach. There is a good anchorage just around this point to the north of the beach.

Escanaba is a friendly city, and supermarkets and restaurants are easily within walking distance of the harbor. The Ludington House Hotel has long been noted for the excellence of its cuisine, and it has been rejuvenated recently by new owners.

Escanaba also boasts a very active yacht club, and members are normally available for local advice.

The same is true 6½ miles further north on Little Bay de Noc at the charming port of Gladstone, which was named for the famed Prime Minister of England.

The deep water channel from Escanaba to Gladstone varies in width from ¾ of a mile to a mile and a half with depths from 26 to 56 feet. A northerly course will take you to port of the R10 bell buoy just northeast of Escanaba and will clear Squaw Point Light, which is a flashing white light on a tower 40 feet high.

The Gladstone breakwater is marked by a light mounted 11 feet high on a wood pole. When Squaw Point Light and Gladstone Pierhead Light are abeam on either hand, a course of 303° will carry you to the yacht harbor entrance.

The yacht basin is about 250 feet by 400 feet, and the north and east sides are lined with docks maintained by the Michigan Waterways Commission. Water, fuel, and electricity are available, and there are showers and toilet facilities along with telephone. An excellent swimming beach adjoins the basin, and the shopping district is within easy walking distance of the harbor.

The Gladstone Yacht Club is a do-it-yourself project, but members will prove to be the most friendly and hospitable of any on the Great Lakes. They are always happy to welcome visiting yachtsmen.

Some of the most beautiful waters and the best fishing for bass and pike are found in Ogontz Bay at the upper end of Little Bay de Noc. The beauty of the environment and the friendliness of the twin harbors at Gladstone and Escanaba should persuade the cruising yachtsmen to spend several days in the area.

The next harbors available on the west shore of Green Bay lie 55 miles to the southwest at Marinette and Menominee. There are two small harbors en route at Ford River and Cedar River, but they are only accessible to boats drawing less than 3 feet.

Marinette and Menominee lie opposite each other astride the Menominee River which is the northern boundary between Wisconsin and Michigan. Both have fine marina facilities.

The Menominee yacht basin is one mile northwest of the outer light at the commercial harbor entrance. It consists of a basin enclosed by a concrete breakwater extending 500 feet out from shore and 1400 feet parallel to the shore with a 100-foot entrance gap at the southeast corner. A red flashing light 21 feet high is on a post at the end of the outer seawall. The entrance may be safely approached from any direction from northwest clockwise

ESCANABA
(Michigan Dept. of Natural Resources photo)

City
Marina

Anchorage

N

GLADSTONE

(Michigan Department of Natural Resources photo)

City
Marina

Anchorage

N

to southeast, and the course through the gap is 307° True. The dockmaster on duty will welcome visiting yachtsmen and assign overnight tie-ups. All facilities are available, including gasoline, water, ice, electricity, pump-out, and there are also very good restroom and shower facilities.

The marina at Marinette is now called the Menominee River Marina and is located 2⅛ miles upstream from the entrance to the commercial harbor. Formerly Reimer's, it has been expanded and improved by a new owner at a reported investment of $1.5 million.

The channel entrance is marked by a flashing red light and a red triangular day mark on a red skeleton tower on the end of the north pier; and a similar flashing light and black square day mark on a white pole on the end of the south breakwater. The course up the channel is 245° True. There is one bridge which opens on command up until 11:00 p.m. Proceed past the yards of the Marinette Marine Company and into the marina.

The marina has 22 piers and full services, including restrooms, water, washer, dryer, ships store with complete marine inventory; all in all, one of the nicest facilities on the lakes.

There is an excellent municipal marina nearby, so you have the choice of two places. A new marina is under construction, and it is hoped it will be ready for the 1984 season.

The shopping areas of both Marinette and Menominee are readily available to both harbors and will provide an excellent place for visitors to restock.

The Marinette/Menominee harbors are best visited from the other shore of Green Bay, since the prevailing south and southwest winds will generally offer a fine reaching voyage from Sturgeon Bay, Egg Harbor, Fish Creek, or Ephraim.

Nearby is Green Island, uninhabited, which offers a good anchorage in the lee of whatever winds are about that particular day, and it is a fine place for a swim or picnic lunch or just exploring ashore.

Chambers Island is also readily available for the same purposes from either Marinette or Menominee, and the varied opportunities offered readily at hand from these two harbors also make them an excellent place to spend several days.

There are excellent restaurants ashore, plus hospitals and an airport where scheduled service is available to Green Bay and points beyond. This also makes this an excellent place to change crews.

A southeast hitch of about 15 miles will bring the cruising sailor back to Sturgeon Bay from whence we started. There may be reasons why a visitor will wish to proceed south into the lower areas of Green Bay, and in that case, we will treat that area in the next chapter.

UPRIVER HARBOR. The Oconto Yacht Harbor lies up the Oconto River, and it is rather tricky navigating the channel. Sailors are advised to be cautious. *Robert McCoy photo*

Public
Dock

N

MARINETTE
(Wisconsin Division of Tourism photo)

City Marina

Anchorage

MENOMINEE

(Michigan Department of Natural Resources photo)

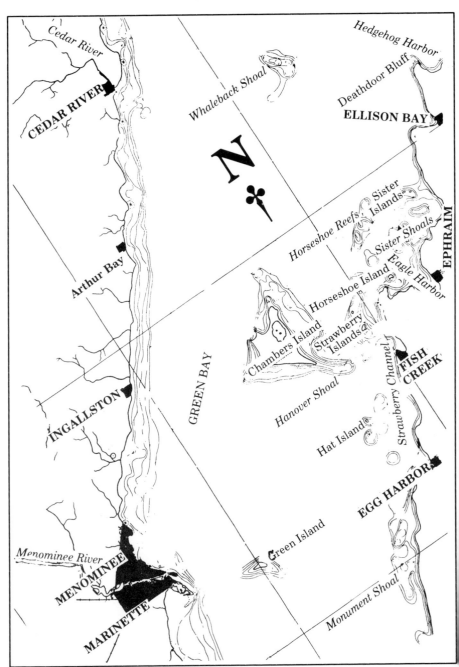

15

LOWER GREEN BAY

There is little to interest the sailor in lower Green Bay except for a visit to the city of Green Bay itself. Sailing waters disappear gradually as you proceed south from Sturgeon Bay or Marinette/Menominee, and visitors are advised to stick close to the channel once they pass the harbor entrance lighthouse 11 miles out of Green Bay.

There are dangerous reefs all along the west shore from Marinette to Green Bay, the most prominent of which is the Peshtigo Reef almost due south from Green Island, and while this is marked by a 72-foot light tower at the east end of the reef, even local sailors have problems going aground in this area.

The other problem in sailing in lower Green Bay is an almost complete absence of harbors of refuge once you leave the Sturgeon Bay and Marinette areas. The only possible exception is the harbor in the river at Oconto. The entrance to the river is protected by piers on both the north and south, and there is an ample mooring basin inside the breakwaters, along with 300 feet of dock space with 7 to 8 feet of water. Dockage is also available at the Oconto Yacht Club, one mile inside the river mouth. There, gas and other supplies are available, and the yacht club itself is in operation 12 months of the year.

The ends of the north and south piers are marked by flashing lights. The only problem in the area is the wreck of a steamer lying 3¾ miles due south from the pierhead light with a depth of 4 feet over it. It is marked by a red nun.

There is also shelter available from northerly winds behind Longtail Point off the west shore near the south end of Green Bay, but boats drawing over 3 feet should not attempt entry into the harbor formed by the Big Suamico River.

The harbor at Green Bay is a busy, major shipping terminus of the St. Lawrence Seaway. A large island of sand a mile and a half from the Fox River's mouth blocked the entrance in the early shipping days until Congress in 1866 appropriated $75,000 to dredge through what is now known as Grassy Island. The channel was widened and deepened on many occasions since that time until now the channel is maintained at a 24-foot depth.

The Green Bay Yacht Club is located on the port hand just inside the mouth of the Fox River and usually has accommodations available for transients. Full services are offered, along with a hospitable bar and occasional meal service.

Proceeding under the scenic Tower Drive Bridge, which has a vertical clearance of 114 feet, the visitor will pass through a railroad bridge and will note a Holiday Inn on the port side of the river where tie-ups are available along the face of the dock.

Complete marine services are available at the Zeller Marine Mart on the east bank of the river past the three automobile bridges in downtown Green Bay. It has a 25-ton travelift and a good stock of yacht supplies.

From here the Fox River proceeds through 17 locks in a length of 37 miles to Lake Winnebago. This is an interesting trip for shoal draft craft, and the scenery is delightful. But operation of the locks beyond the 1984 boating season is in question. An emergency appropriation was approved by Congress in the last week of its 1983 session, providing sufficient funds for the U. S. Corps of Engineers to operate the locks for one more year, but this was with the understanding that in October 1984 the state of Wisconsin would have to assume responsibility for their continued operation. This matter is currently in limbo.

There are many attractions for the tourist in the Green Bay area, sufficient to make the trip through lower Green Bay to the city worthwhile. Highlighting these are the Green Bay Packers Hall of Fame adjoining Packer headquarters and Lambeau Field where the Packers play; the National Railroad Museum, a storehouse of memorabilia from the steam era of railroading; and Heritage Hill History Park where a number of original buildings from the early settlement of Green Bay have been restored.

Detailed information is available from the Green Bay Visitor's Bureau.

A new entry on the harbor scene in Green Bay is a giant smokestack erected by the Fort Howard Paper Company, which is lighted at the top and at mid-point by 24-hour strobe lights. These provide a general aiming point for the harbor as they are visible at least 25 miles away. But the channel markings should be followed exactly from entrance light all the way into the harbor as there is shoal water just outside the channel in a number of areas.

OPEN WIDE. The Fox River opens its mouth wide as it pours into Green Bay. This picture was taken in 1976 before the bridge for Interstate 43 was constructed. *Robert McCoy photo*

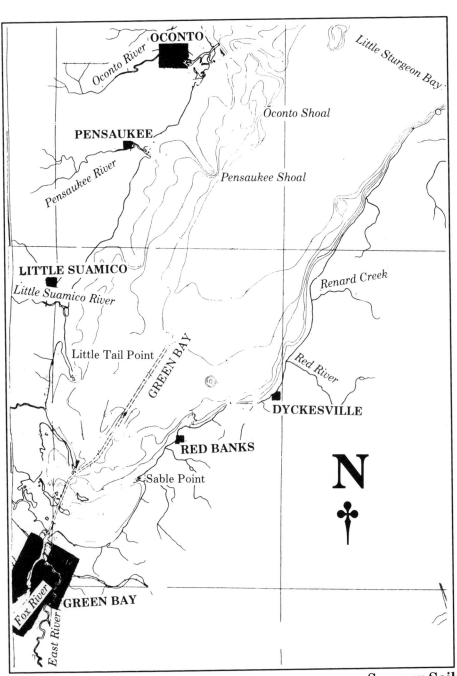

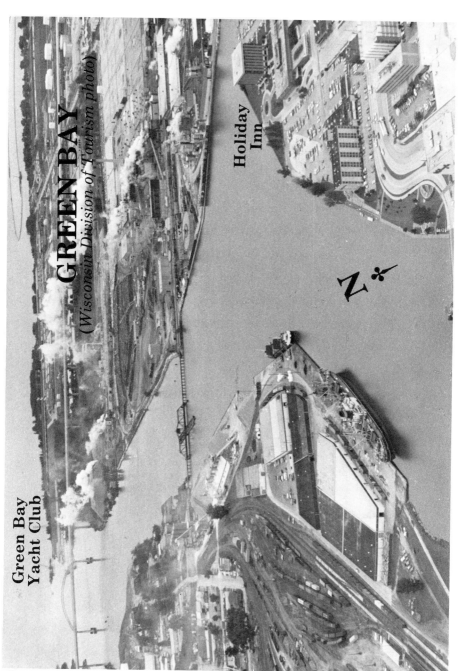

GREEN BAY
(Wisconsin Division of Tourism photo)

Holiday Inn

Green Bay
Yacht Club

SAILING, SAILING. During the summer months, Green Bay offers some of the most ideal conditions for sailing. Several yacht clubs located in various ports along the bay sponsor racing events throughout the season. *Courtesy Door County Advocate*

Summer Sail

16

SAIL RACING
ON GREEN BAY

There are a number of active yacht clubs on Green Bay, all of which sponsor one or more sail racing events during the summer. Most of them welcome visiting yachtsmen as participants.

The Green Bay Yachting Association co-ordinates the sail racing schedule and designates a number of these events to count in a boat of the year series. The best source of information on the schedule is Sue Holloway at Palmer Johnson in Sturgeon Bay. Sue and her husband George are active participants in the racing scene, and she serves as secretary of the Green Bay Yachting Association. The GBYA is a member of the Lake Michigan Yachting Association and frequently hosts the LMYA championships on Green Bay.

Cruising class races are sponsored by the Sturgeon Bay Yacht Club, the Egg Harbor Yacht Club, the Ephraim Yacht Club, the Escanaba Yacht Club, and the Marinette/Menominee Yacht Club. Each of these have their own club races during the season, and each sponsors at least one race for the GBYA boat of the year series.

One of these is an overnight race.

The so-called 100-miler is probably the best known of the races on Green Bay. Sponsored by the Marinette/ Menominee Yacht Club, it is always held the weekend after conclusion of the Chicago/Mackinac race and normally attracts a number of the yachts which are on their way home from Mackinac.

There are active small boat fleets at Sturgeon Bay, Ephraim, Marinette/Menominee, and in the Green Bay area, notably the Windjammers Club headquartered at the Eagles Nest on the southeast corner of Green Bay. The Green Bay Yacht Club is primarily a power boat club, given the limitations on availability of sailing water at the lower end of the bay.

All of the harbors on Green Bay have launching facilities so small boat sailors wishing to participate in any of these events can readily trailer their craft to any given area.

Visiting sailors wishing to participate in any of these racing events are advised, however, to contact the host club in advance to make necessary arrangements.

17

AN IDEAL CRUISE

This book would not be complete without a recommendation for my idea of an ideal cruise of Green Bay. These suggestions will be for a two week stay in these beautiful waters, although I will also indicate how it could be reduced to a week or 10 days.

Let's begin with a landfall at the entrance to the Sturgeon Bay and Lake Michigan Ship Canal and proceed from there into Sturgeon Bay itself. Let's plan to tie up at either the Sturgeon Bay Yacht Club or across the harbor at Palmer Johnson shipyard. In the former case, the Baudhuin Yacht Harbor is available next door which carries a full supply of charts in case you will be needing any of those suggested earlier in this book. The alternate tie-up at Palmer Johnson is suggested for those sailors who might want to inspect some of the beautiful custom yachts under construction or being fitted out in the yard. Palmer Johnson is also more convenient to the retail shopping center of Sturgeon Bay.

For art lovers, I might suggest one point of interest in Sturgeon Bay. The Miller Art Gallery, attached to the Door County Library, is a short four blocks from the Palmer Johnson docks. There are continuous changes in showings at the gallery along with a very fine permanent

Fl. R. 2.5 sec.

Fl. R. 10 sec.

Fl. G. 4 sec.

Entrance

N

STURGEON BAY
SHIP CANAL

(Harmann photo)

collection featuring Wisconsin artists, particularly those from Door County.

For those yachtsmen who would prefer anchoring overnight instead of tying up at either of these downtown piers, they can proceed northwest up Sturgeon Bay to Sawyer Harbor, which offers a fine protected anchorage on the port side of Sturgeon Bay.

Our first day is going to be spent crossing Green Bay to the Marinette/Menominee area on the west shore, a distance of 16 miles. As you proceed out through Sturgeon Bay, note the extensive remains of a huge limestone quarry on the northeast shore just inside the point. On the port side, note also the beautiful bluff at Sherwood Point and the lighthouse atop the bluff which was the last one to be converted to automatic operation on the Great Lakes.

Moving out into the bay, you will begin to notice the picturesque scenery of the Green Bay side of Door County, marked by a succession of headlands alternating with beautiful little harbors where the resort villages are located. This is a good time also to get your initial bearings for sailing on Green Bay. Note that the Door County shoreline extends in a northeasterly direction, thus our heading for crossing the bay from Sturgeon Bay to Marinette/Menominee is north/northwest, 330° magnetic. Given the prevailing southwesterly winds, it should be a lazy, placid reach.

Most of our daily jaunts will be relatively short, in the area of 15 to 25 miles each, and therefore, anchorages will be suggested for a mid-day soiree, including swimming and lunch, usually ashore at one of the many fine eateries in the area.

On our way from Sturgeon Bay to Marinette/Menominee, let's stop then off Green Island which is about three quarters of the way across. Good holding is available on all sides of the island. We will choose whichever side is in the lee.

Proceeding on into the twin cities which lie astride the Menominee River, we have a choice of two excellent marinas. The first is a privately maintained facility about a mile up river from the harbor entrance which has been expanded considerably in recent years as described in Chapter 14. The other choice is the public facility at Menominee which lies just inside a breakwater just north of the main harbor entrance. Both of these marinas have full services, and transient boats are welcomed.

Since we presumably stocked up in Sturgeon Bay, we have no particular reason to spend more than one night in the Marinette/Menominee area, so we will proceed on the second day to cross the bay again to the interesting port at Fish Creek, a distance of about 18 miles.

But just as on the previous day, we will schedule a mid-day stop-over at Chambers Island which is a little over half way across the bay. We will choose the beautiful bay at the north end of Chambers for our swim and lunch, unless there are strong northerly winds. In that case, we will anchor off the south shore.

There is one navigational marker to note on the way from Marinette/Menominee to Chambers Island, and that is a black bell buoy at the end of the reef extending west from Chambers Island. This should be given good berth when proceeding to the anchorage at the north end or to the south side of the island also. You will notice a light on a 97-foot tower at the northwest corner of the island, but there is good water off that point. After rounding that point, proceed due east until the center of the harbor opens, then proceed in to shore. This is a fine sandy beach, and the anchor can be dropped quite close in.

We do have some navigational problems, however, in proceeding from this north bay of Chambers Island to Fish Creek.

First, the black bell buoy well off the northern tip of the island must be left to starboard. It marks the end of a shoal that extends a good two miles out from the island.

After rounding this buoy, we will proceed southeast down through the channel between Chambers Island and the Strawberries. Here we must be aware of the red nun at the eastern end of Hanover Shoal at the southeast corner

Sawyer Harbor

Snug Harbor

Palmer Johnson

Sturgeon Bay Yacht Club

N

STURGEON BAY

(Harmann photo)

HORSESHOE ISLAND. This picturesque island in Eagle Harbor often serves as a mark on the course for sailing races. Its natural harbor also provides fine protection for anchoring over night or for a swim and lunch.

Harmann photo

of Chambers Island. This marks the end of a shoal which again extends almost two miles out from shore.

After leaving red nun #8 to starboard, we must also check for a black can off a reef extending south from the Strawberry Islands. This must be left to port after which we can proceed right on into Fish Creek.

At Fish Creek, we will have a choice of tying up at the Alibi Dock, which is privately operated, or at the public dock. There is also good holding at anchor well into the harbor where a number of private moorings are maintained.

I suggest seeing one of the presentations of the Peninsula Players which are offered every night of the week except Monday. Reservations can be made ahead of time from Sturgeon Bay or Marinette/Menominee by telephoning 414-868-3287. Transportation will be arranged by the Players.

On our third day, we will take a leisurely sail up the Door County coast, dropping anchor at Horseshoe Island or Shanty Bay in Eagle Harbor for a swim and lunch, then overnighting in picturesque Ellison Bay at the Cedar Lodge Resort.

I should remark at this time that, if your first mate is ready for relief in the galley, two excellent places to go ashore for dinner are the C & C Club in Fish Creek or the John Ellison Supper Club in Ellison Bay. You might also want to try a fishboil at the Viking Restaurant in Ellison Bay, and be sure to drop in and look over the old time general store across the street on the main corner.

We now proceed to the very unique Washington Island where we will spend a little time. For this purpose, we will make our first stop at Detroit Harbor on the southwest corner of the island where we can either tie up at one of three marinas or anchor out in Peterson Bay. This is only a short haul of a little over 10 miles, and we will plan to arrive by early afternoon so we can go ashore and buy some fresh whitefish for dinner.

At any rate, upon arrival we should use a telephone to call Vi's taxi cab and have her take us on a lecture tour of the island. Vi will be glad to drop us off at any of a number of local pubs where we can have a shot of bitters washed down by beer and get a card signifying our membership in the club.

Washington Island is worth another day's stay at either Detroit Harbor or Peterson Bay, for there is excellent fishing available, or the ladies might want to visit the island's museum and/or art gallery.

One of the evening meals on these fourth or fifth days should be fresh whitefish, whether it is broiled aboard or prepared in a local restaurant, and for appetizers, an ample helping of whitefish livers.

From Detroit Harbor, we will now proceed up the west shore of Washington Island, north along the chain of islands leading to the Garden Peninsula of Michigan.

And, as on other occasions, there are two islands which will provide convenient mid-day respites. Either the cove on the north end of St. Martin Island or the picturesque harbor at the northeast corner of Summer Island will do. The latter, however, is a bit out of our way, for we plan to proceed up the west coast of the Garden Peninsula to Burnt Bluff, a most pleasant overnight stopping point which is now owned and operated by Tim Minahan. Be sure and tell Tim I sent you.

An excursion ashore is recommended at Burnt Bluff, particularly the stone quarry where Indian paintings still exist on the rock faces of the quarry.

I should note that this is a passage of about 28 miles, but given the prevailing southwesterly winds on Green Bay or even a brisk northwester, it is a delightful sail, one which I have often made under spinnaker.

There is a choice of overnight harbors in this area and if Tim's place is full, it is only four miles up the pike to the beautiful Snail Harbor at Fayette, although I had planned to make this a luncheon stop the next day if we over-nighted at Burnt Bluff.

Whether we stay at Burnt Bluff or at Fayette, however, we will proceed another four miles north the next day to the natural harbor at South River Bay. This is the mid-point of our cruise and an idyllic spot to spend a day at anchor and at rest.

Anchorage

Channel <------ Entrance

N

JACKSON HARBOR

(Harmann photo)

Ferry Dock

Public Dock

ST. MARTIN
ISLAND
(Robert McCoy photo)

St. Martin Island
Lighthouse

From South River Bay we are now going to cross Big Bay de Noc into the Little Bay and then proceed up to the marina at Escanaba.

It is about 20 miles to the shoals off the south end of Stonington Point, marked by a red bell buoy off Corona shoal. We do not have to round the Minneapolis shoal lighthouse before proceeding into Little Bay de Noc, but we will leave the Corona Shoal bell buoy to starboard before heading on into the Little Bay.

At this point, we should also look for the black bell buoy marking the port side of the Little Bay de Noc channel and head straight north for the R8A bell buoy in the center of the channel off Escanaba.

From the Corona Shoal bell buoy, it is another 10 miles to the harbor at Escanaba. After passing the R8A bell buoy, continue straight north until the marina entrance opens up on the port side.

You will like the facilities and the friendly people at the headquarters of the Escanaba Yacht Club. The same is true of the Gladstone Yacht Club in the harbor of the same name another 7 miles north. I recommend proceeding up Little Bay de Noc to Gladstone for a day's stay in that area, particularly if you have any fishing in mind.

From either Gladstone or Escanaba, we will now sail south through Little Bay de Noc, leave the Minneapolis Shoal lighthouse to port, and cruise another 14 miles southeast to Jackson Harbor on Washington Island; a total of 25 miles from Escanaba. At this point, go back and read the instructions for making port at Jackson Harbor.

This is a most unique and enjoyable harbor, and we will spend day 11 here after arriving on day 10, if only to purchase some fresh whitefish right off one of the fishing boats and have it filleted before our very eyes. Another serving of whitefish livers may also be in order.

At Jackson Harbor, you should visit the Dune Nature Preserve area up the road and to your left. It has been preserved like the Ridges Sanctuary by private funding. There is a delightful sand beach in the preserve area in addition.

And if you didn't do so when we visited Detroit Harbor, use the telephone at the dock and call Vi's taxi cab for a tour of the island. She will be happy to drop you off at Carly's bar for a shot of bitters and pick you up sometime later.

I suggest spending the 11th day of our two-week cruise at Jackson Harbor because of the uniqueness of the area.

On the 12th, we will take off for Sister Bay, which includes a 5-mile reach across the northern end of Washington Island to Boyer Bluff, then an 18-mile leg to Sister Bay. We will either tie up at the village dock or anchor behind the breakwater. An alternative is the Anchor Marina, particularly if you are in need of any services from that facility.

A luncheon of Swedish pancakes at Al Johnson's restaurant is a must in Sister Bay, and you might want to consider dinner ashore at the Sister Bay Bowl. Either breakfast or luncheon ashore can be accommodated in Sister Bay on day 13 since our next leg to Egg Harbor is a short one. We will hug the shore as we proceed south from Sister Bay past Eagle Bluff, head down through the Strawberry Channel right into Egg Harbor, a total distance of less than 15 miles.

You will want to walk up the hill to this charming village, stop in the bar at The Blue Iris (formerly the Thimbleberry Inn) for a drink, and consider dinner there or up the street at Tony's Stage Station Italian restaurant, or even a little further up the street at Casey's.

Hopefully, we have arrived in Egg Harbor on a weekend for concerts of either modern jazz or chamber music which are available at the Birch Creek Music School on Friday and Saturday nights. If you didn't get to see a performance of the Peninsula Players early in our cruise, their summer theatre is also just a few miles up the highway from Egg Harbor.

Egg Harbor, then, is our last port of call on our two-week cruise of Green Bay, with day 14 reserved for returning to Sturgeon Bay and preparing to transit the canal on your way back to your home port.

CHAMBERS ISLAND

(Robert McCoy photo)

DEATHDOOR BLUFF

(Robert McCoy photo)

If it is necessary for you to limit your Green Bay cruise to a 9-day period, including two weekends, I would make the following suggestions:

Day 1, Sturgeon Bay or Sawyer Harbor; day 2, Marinette/Menominee; day 3, Ellison Bay; day 4, Detroit Harbor on Washington Island; day 5, Burnt Bluff; day 6, Escanaba; day 7, Jackson Harbor back on Washington Island; day 8, Egg Harbor; and day 9, return to Sturgeon Bay.

I have finished both of these suggested cruises at my home port of Egg Harbor for a specific reason.

When you reach the village dock there, please look me up, and I will be happy to personally autograph your copy of this book.

My boat's name is *Cheers!*

A FITTING END. Sunsets over Green Bay are usually very beautiful. Among the boats here is the author's yacht *Cheers* **tied up in its slip at Egg Harbor.** *Peggy Eagan photo*

POTOWATOMI LIGHT
ROCK ISLAND

(Harmann photo)

Summer Sail

APPENDIX

CHRONOLOGY

425,000,000 B.C. — Silurian Sea inundates Great Lakes Basin, creates Niagara Escarpment.

30,000 B.C.— Wisconsin Glacier covers Upper Michigan, northern Wisconsin.

8,000 B.C. — Copper Indian culture appears along shores of Green Bay.

1634 — Jean Nicolet lands at Red Banks on Green Bay, claims Wisconsin for France.

1671 — Fr. Claude Allouez establishes mission on Fox River at *Rapides des Pere*.

1679 — Robert de La Salle sails *The Griffon* to Rock Island; ship sank in late autumn storm.

1754 - 1763 — French and Indian Wars.

1763 — Wisconsin becomes British territory.

1775 - 1783 — American Revolution.

1787 — Wisconsin becomes part of Northwest Territory of United States.

1812 - 1814 — War of 1812.

1816 — British finally leave Wisconsin; Ft. Howard established at mouth of Fox River.

1825 — Opening of Erie Canal; beginning of Great Lakes shipping.

1836 — Territory of Wisconsin formally established.

1848 — Statehood.

1854 — GOP founded in Ripon.

1855 — Opening of Soo Locks.

1861 - 1865 — Civil War.

1882 - Opening of Sturgeon Bay Ship Canal.

1914 - 1918 — World War I.

1919 — Curly Lambeau and George W. Calhoun found Green Bay Packers professional football team; oldest pro team in NFL.

1941 - 1945 — World War II.

1959 — Opening of St. Lawrence Seaway.

STONE QUARRIES

One of the spectacular sites in cruising Green Bay are the numerous remains of huge stone quarries, memorials to what was known as the "Golden Age of Stone" in the area.

Limestone quarried from the Niagara Escarpment in Door County helped build some of the finest harbors on Lake Michigan, hundreds of beautiful and enduring buildings, and provided solid road beds for railroads and highways.

It all began in 1832 when the U. S. government opened a quarry at the foot of the bluff overlooking Sawyer Harbor on the west shore of Sturgeon Bay. Stone was needed for a harbor project at the southern end of Lake Michigan, and Secretary of the Treasury Levi Woodbury approved the establishment of a "government reservation" of 100 acres of land at the mouth of Sturgeon Bay "for the purpose of providing good stone in all weather."

Small quarries developed along both sides of Sturgeon Bay, several of them converting the rock into lime for the building trade. By 1870, one of these quarries was burning and selling more than 1,000 kegs of lime a year.

The boom in quarrying really started, however, with the opening of the Sturgeon Bay canal for heavy traffic in the 1880s, providing a shorter route to the ports on Lake Michigan. In the 1890s, crushing operations were added to the quarries, providing gravel for the construction of railroads and highways in that part of Wisconsin.

Curiously, the stone quarry business also led to the development of the shipbuilding industry in Sturgeon Bay. Leathem and Smith Company, being heavily engaged in quarrying, decided to begin building ships in which to carry the stone to market.

The remains of the largest stone quarry on the Great Lakes are seen along the northeast shore of Sturgeon Bay near its mouth with Green Bay.

The dolomite rock also was the raw material for the production of lime, used both in agriculture and in the building industry. To produce lime, the dolomite is crushed, then heated to drive off carbon dioxide. This reduces the volume by about one half. The lime was also used as a flux in iron ore furnaces. This made for a boom industry in the smelting of Upper Peninsula iron ore at the port of Fayette on the Garden Peninsula of Michigan in the latter part of the 19th century. The availability of lime from the nearby quarry at Burnt Bluff and the charcoal made from the forests in the area were the raw materials for a prosperous smelting industry at Fayette in those times. The state of Michigan has reconstructed the kilns and smelting furnaces in the state park at Fayette.

The quarries also present a fascinating picture of the geological history of the Niagara Escarpment with their layers upon layers of dolomite rock deposited there millions of years ago.

Sailors are encouraged to take a trip ashore to view the quarries, particularly at Burnt Bluff on the Garden Peninsula, or on Big Summer Island.

MYSTERY SHIP
ALVIN CLARK

THE MYSTERY SHIP

Vivid memories of the days of the sailing schooners will be revived by a visit to the so-called *Mystery Ship* now docked in Menominee.

The mystery began when commercial fishermen complained about losing nets when they became entangled with an underwater object off the west side of Chambers Island. They asked Frank Hoffman, a diver from Egg Harbor, to investigate. What Frank found was a sailing schooner in near perfect condition resting upright on the bottom of the bay in some 110 feet of water.

Hoffman owned and operated a tavern in Egg Harbor, which was a hangout for divers, and the more they talked about the *Mystery Ship* over a few beers, the more they became interested in trying to learn more about the vessel. They began weekend dives in the area and brought up a number of articles from the sunken ship.

Jim Quinn, director of the museum in Green Bay and himself a professional diver, joined the group and began a scientific study of the ship and its treasures, particularly an attempt to identify it. At this point, Hoffman and his buddies began to talk about the possibility of raising the ship and restoring it as a museum in itself.

What started out as weekend fun and adventure now became a major operation. Hoffman mortgaged and finally sold his tavern to help finance the project. Getting cables tunnelled under the ship and attached to lifting tanks proved to be a tedious process. There were a number of futile attempts to lift the ship intact before the feat was finally accomplished in 1969. And when they finally had the ship afloat, the problems were just beginning.

Timbers and deck plates and spars and fittings like those of the *Mystery Ship* had been beautifully preserved while it was under water, but now that it was exposed to the air it became a race against time to apply various preservatives to prevent deterioration. And all this proved expensive. Hoffman begged, borrowed, and, yes, almost stole to convert his schooner into a tourist attraction.

Meanwhile, Quinn, after a great deal of research, was able to identify the schooner as the *Alvin Clark*, a 113-foot sailing ship which had gone down with a full load of lumber during a storm in 1864.

The large number of sunken wrecks in Green Bay waters are an added attraction for sailors who are also scuba divers. Maps are available locating and indentifying a number of them, and equipment for diving is readily available in a number of ports.

There is a diving school on the shore near Gill's Rock at the tip of the Peninsula, and charter diving trips to various wrecks in Death's Door Passage are operated from there.

One notable wreck which has never been found, however, is that of *The Griffon*, one of the earliest large schooners on the Great Lakes. It disappeared with a valuable load of furs on its way to Mackinac Island. It is believed to have founderd in the Washington Island area, but it has never been located.

The *Alvin Clark* may be visited from a public dock on the Michigan side of the Menominee River. Any sailors visiting that port should take the time to do so.

SUNKEN TREASURE. These are some of the artifacts brought up from the sunken schooner *Alvin Clark*. The largest crock, second from the right, contained cheese that, although it had been resting at the bottom of Green Bay for over 100 years, was still good. The *Mystery Ship*, as the *Alvin Clark* was called, is now a museum located in Menominee, Michigan.
Courtesy of the Neville Museum

POVERTY ISLAND
TREASURE TROVE

The legend of the Poverty Island treasure trove has stirred imaginations for over a century. Reputedly the richest sunken treasure in the Great Lakes and one of the richest in North America, the trove remains surrounded in mystery.

The ship carrying the treasure continues to be nameless; the nation supplying its contents has never been precisely identified; and the treasure's final destination and use still are undetermined.

Poverty Island is a small rocky outcrop in the northeastern part of the island chain that stretches from the Door Peninsula of Wisconsin to the Garden Peninsula of Michigan. Dangerous shoals lie about it.

In August of 1864 while the Civil War raged further south, what seems to have been a smuggling vessel, which may have had a profound impact on the future of the Confederacy, slipped through the Straits of Mackinac bound for the Poverty Island Passage and the harbor of Escanaba. Several accounts state the ship was carrying $5 million in gold bullion. After this fact, however, the fate of the treasure, crew, and ship becomes more speculative. The legend describes, that as the vessel neared the Poverty Island area, its captain became concerned. He knew other vessels were following his route in what was generally considered a heyday in Great Lakes shipping, and he wanted utmost secrecy. He also knew pirates were about. Thus, when a sleek cutter began pursuing his boat, gradually drawing closer, the captain came to a resolute decision. He ordered his crew to chain together the five chests containing the gold and throw the chests overboard. Later, according to one report, the ship was boarded by the pirates and afterwards burned and sunk.

The name of the ship may never be known. But the mysterious gold supplier and the treasure's use and destination might be learned if the cache is discovered.

Meanwhile, conjecture about these mysteries livens conversation in upper Green Bay ports like Escanaba, Gladstone, and Fairport. "Was the gold supplier Great Britain, secret ally of the Confederacy?" the question is asked. "Was the gold to be smuggled through Michigan and Wisconsin to the Mississippi River, and thence to some river port, and on to Richmond by rail?" "Or was it going the other way to Canada to buy weapons?" Anyone's guess is as good as another's — till the Poverty Island treasure is raised.

THE GRIFFON

In 1678, Rene-Robert Cavalier de La Salle thought to enter the fur trade in the Great Lakes region against the orders of his superiors in Montreal. His first task was to construct a ship, *The Griffon*, above Niagara Falls in Lake Erie.

The Griffon set sail the next year for the islands that separated Green Bay from Lake Michigan.

An archeological dig by Ronald and Carol Mason of Lawrence University in Appleton, Wisconsin has indicated that La Salle's ship and crew rendezvoused with area Indians on Rock Island. After taking on a full load of furs, the ship set sail for the East but was never heard from again.

Some authorities speculate *The Griffon* sank in a storm before reaching the Straits of Mackinac. Others think it was overloaded, and because it was built with green wood, it became water-logged and went down. The possibility that it ran aground and was abandoned has been ruled out because no trace of the crew was ever found.

No matter what caused the disappearance of *The Griffon*, historians are relatively certain that it vanished in northern Lake Michigan, never reaching Lake Huron. The reasoning behind this theory is the location of the Jesuit mission at St. Ignace on the north shore of the Straits of Mackinac. *The Griffon* would have had to sail past the mission and more than likely would have been seen if it had, whether passing in the day or night.

Some authorities believe *The Griffon* sank near Washington Island shortly after its departure, while others feel it reached Beaver Island before going down. The most likely possibility is it disappeared near Seul Choix Point on Michigan's Upper Peninsula. Until it is actually found, this is all conjecture.

A Big Tow. Greetings from Sturgeon Bay, Wis.

BIG TOW. This 1911 picture postcard depicts a tug pulling six schooners through the Sturgeon Bay Ship Canal. The freighters are under full sail to assist the tug but could not navigate the canal without help.
Courtesy Chan Harris, Door County Advocate

CHERRY TRAIN TOUR. Here's a fun way for the family to see Washington Island. Take a ride on Wisconsin Tour Trains' Cherry Train and view the island close up. Another way is to take Vi's Taxi.

Harmann photo

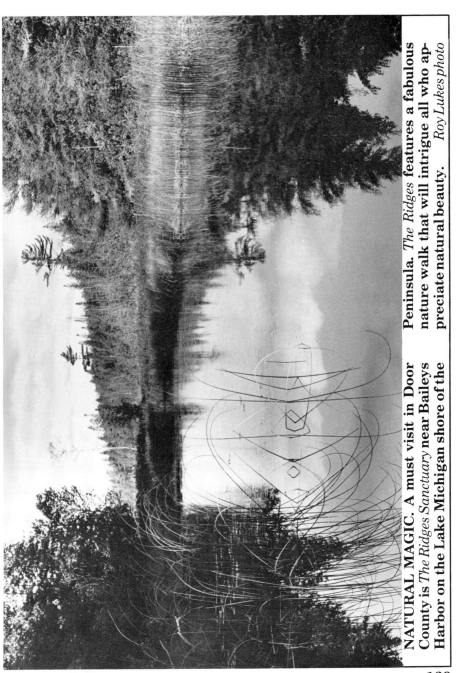

NATURAL MAGIC. A must visit in Door County is *The Ridges Sanctuary* near Baileys Harbor on the Lake Michigan shore of the Peninsula. *The Ridges* features a fabulous nature walk that will intrigue all who appreciate natural beauty. *Roy Lukes photo*

"I CHRISTEN THEE. . ." Peterson Ship Builders of Sturgeon Bay constructs ships of all kinds and all sizes. Launchings such as this one are almost considered a spectator sport in area.

Harmann photo

SWING IT! One of the many summertime entertainment features of Door County is the Birch Creek Music School's jazz sessions. The musicians and the Peninsula Players outdoor theatre provide some of the best live entertainment anywhere.

Courtesy of the Door County Advocate

SHE'S A BEAUTY. The gaff-rigged sloop, *The Algonquin*, was the pride of Arthur C. Neville in the early days of sailing on Green Bay. The Green Bay Museum is named for him. *Neville Museum photo*

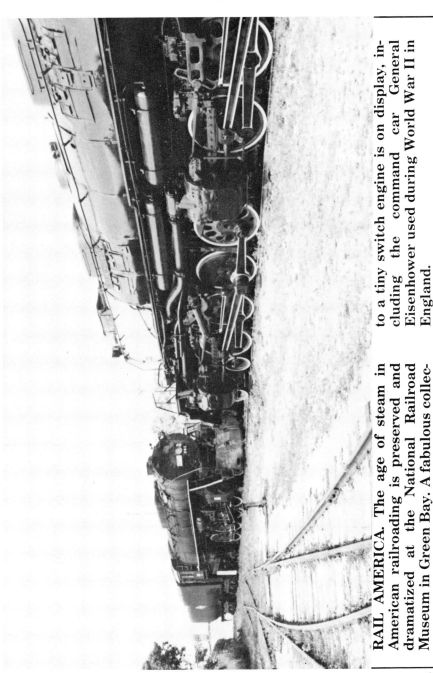

RAIL AMERICA. The age of steam in American railroading is preserved and dramatized at the National Railroad Museum in Green Bay. A fabulous collection of steam locomotives from the *Big Boy* to a tiny switch engine is on display, including the command car General Eisenhower used during World War II in England.

Courtesy Green Bay Visitors Bureau

NEW GREEN BAY MUSEUM. The new $5 million Neville Public Museum was opened in Green Bay in 1983 and features an elaborate diorama, "On the Shore of the Inland Sea," a geological and human history of the area. It's well worth a visit in Green Bay.

Courtesy Green Bay Visitors Bureau

LIVING HISTORY PARK. Heritage Hill State Park at Green Bay stands on the site of the first settlement in the entire area. A number of buildings 150 years old or more have been moved to the park and restored there. The story of the settlement of this region is told in living history.

Courtesy Green Bay Visitors Bureau

LAMBEAU FIELD. This is the home of the Green Bay Packers, a municipal stadium seating some 56,000 fans. The stadium is sold out every year on a season ticket basis. There is adjacent parking for 6,000 vehicles. *Courtesy Green Bay Visitors Bureau*

WILDLIFE SANCTUARY. A city park on the shore of Green Bay has been developed into a tourist attraction as a wildlife sanctuary where native animals and birds can be seen in their natural element.

With the gradual clean up of the waters from the Fox River draining into lower Green Bay, the opening of a swimming beach there is becoming a possibility again. *Courtesy Green Bay Visitors Bureau*

INDEX

A

B

C

C & C Club — 40, 44, 54, 119
Cap's Marina — 68
Carly's Bar — 124
Casey's Inn — 40, 124
Catholic Diocese of Green Bay — 53
Cedar Grove Resort Marina — 61, 63
Cedar Lodge Resort — 119
Cedar River — 97
Chambers Island — 51, 53, 100, 116, 119
Cheers — 9, 127
Chicago — 16, 29, 76, 82, 83, 85
Chicago-Mackinac Race — 112
Chippewa Indians — 89
Claflin, Increase — 43, 51
Clearing, The — 14
Congress, U. S. — 30, 106
Cornell, Jim — 82
Corona Shoal — 123
Corps of Engineers — 106
Crash of 1929 — 53

D

Deathdoor Bluff — 55, 66
Death's Door Passage (*also Porte des Morts*) — 9, 65, 66, 75
Demariness, Sara — 39
Demariness, Tony — 39
Detroit Harbor — 67, 68, 69, 119, 120, 124, 127
Detroit Island — 67, 68
Door County *Advocate* — 11, 30, 37, 38
Door County Library — 113
Door County Peninsula — 13, 14, 16, 43, 50, 55, 57, 62, 63, 65, 75, 85, 95
Drummond Island — 14
Dune Nature Preserve — 123

E

F

G

H

Horseshoe Reef — 55
Hudson Bay — 50

I

Idlewild Pines Motel — 35
Indian paintings — 120
Insull, Samuel — 53
Iriquois Indians — 65

J - K

Jackson Harbor — 81, 82, 83, 123, 124, 127
Janssen, Greg — 39
Janssen, Jack — 39
John Ellison Supper Club — 62, 119

L

Lake Erie — 14
Lake Huron — 14, 19, 22
Lake Michigan — 9, 11, 14, 15, 16, 17, 19, 21, 22, 29, 30,
    32, 50, 62, 66, 67, 73, 75, 77, 81, 83
Lake Michigan Yachting Association — 111
Lake Nippising — 19
Lake Superior — 13
Lake Winnebago — 20, 106
Lambeau Field (Green Bay) — 107
Lautenbach, Dave — 39
Leland — 16
Little Bay de Noc — 17, 21, 92, 95, 97, 123
Little Summer Island — 86
Lobdell's Point — 68
Longtail Point — 106
Lorain Marine telephone service — 21
Ludington House Hotel — 96
Lukes, Charlotte — 14

Lukes, Roy — 14, 15

M

Mackinac Island — 37, 66, 112
Mackinac, Straits of — *See Straits of Mackinac*
Madison — 83
Manistique — 86
Manitoulin Island — 14
Manson, Bob — 40
Marinette — 29, 54, 97, 100, 105, 112, 115, 119, 127
Marinette Marine Company — 100
Marinette-Menominee Yacht Club — 111, 112,
Marquette (Michigan) — 20
Marquette, Fr. Pierre — 20
Mattawa River — 19
Maxwellton Braes Resort — 77
Menominee — 29, 54, 97, 100, 105, 112, 115, 119, 127
Menominee Indians — 65
Menominee River — 97, 115
Menominee River Marina — 100
Michigan Bridge (Sturgeon Bay) — 31
Michigan Department of Natural Resources — 23, 91
Michigan Waterways Commission — 97
Miller Art Gallery — 113
Milwaukee — 29, 83, 85
Minahan, Tim — 89, 90, 120
Mink River — 75
Minneapolis Shoal — 96, 123
Mississippi River — 20, 83
Montreal — 19
Moorings, The — 35
Mueller, Bob — 39
Mueller, Herb — 39

N

Names, Larry — 9

O

P

Plum Island — 16, 55, 67
Port Door — 32
Porte des Morts Passage (*also Death's Door Passage*)
— 16, 17, 55, 65, 66
Pottowatomi Indians — 65, 66
Pottowatomi Lighthouse — 83
Poverty Island Passage — 17
Precourt, Rob — 9
Prohibition Era — 69

Q

Quo Vadis ferry — 53

R

Rafferty, Dennis — 51
Reimer's marina — 100
Reimer's Reef — 54
Richter, Arnie — 68
Ridges Sanctuary — 14, 77, 123
Rock Awash — 51, 54
Rock Island — 15, 81, 82, 83
Rock Island Passage — 16
Roen, John — 89
Rowleys Bay — 75, 76

S

Sac Bay — 89
Sac Indians — 65
St. Lawrence Seaway — 106
St. Martin Island — 85, 86, 120
St. Martin Island Passage — 16, 17
Sawyer Harbor — 35, 115, 127
Sawyer Point — 35
Seiches — 22

T

Tower Drive Bridge (Green Bay) — 106
Traverse City — 21

U - V

Van's Harbor — 91
Vi's taxi — 69, 82, 119, 124
Viking Restaurant — 62, 119
Villager restaurant — 40

W

Wagon Trail Resort — 75, 76
War of 1812 — 67
Washington schooner — 67
Washington Harbor — 67, 68
Washington Island — 17, 22, 63, 65, 66, 67, 69, 81, 82,
    119, 120, 123, 124, 127
Waverly Shoal — 67
West Channel — 17
Whaleback Shoal — 55
Wickman, W. F. — 67
Windjammers Club — 112
Winnebago Indians — 65, 66
Wisconsin Department of Natural Resources — 21, 22
    Division of Tourism — 22
Wisconsin River — 20, 83

X-Y-Z

Zeller Marine Mart — 106

John B. Torinus

ABOUT THE AUTHOR

John B. Torinus has been a journalist for over 50 years. He began his career with the Green Bay *Press-Gazette* after graduating from Dartmouth College in 1934 and rose through the editorial ranks to the position of executive editor. He took time off to serve as a reserve Army officer in World War II, retiring with the rank of lieutenant colonel. He became editor of the Appleton *Post-Crescent* in 1962, retiring in 1983.

Torinus began sailing when his teenage daughters took sailing lessons at camp and talked him into buying a Flying Scot. From that 19-foot day sailer, he graduated to a Yankee 24, then a Yankee 28, and finally the 33-foot Ranger he now owns.

Torinus and his wife Louise live in De Pere, Wisconsin but have maintained a summer home in Door County for many years. They have six children: four sons and two daughters, all of whom are also sailors and who have crewed for him at various times. The last to do so was his youngest son Mark who jumped ship. He is now pressing his grandchildren into service.

SUMMER SAIL is his second book. He is also the author of **THE PACKER LEGEND: An Inside Look** and **THE PACKER LEGEND: Revised Edition**.